The Phantom of the Opera

by Gaston Leroux

Level 3
(1600-word)

Retold by Nina Wegner

IBC パブリッシング

はじめに

　ラダーシリーズは、「はしご (ladder)」を使って一歩一歩上を目指すように、学習者の実力に合わせ、無理なくステップアップできるよう開発された英文リーダーのシリーズです。

　リーディング力をつけるためには、繰り返したくさん読むこと、いわゆる「多読」がもっとも効果的な学習法であると言われています。多読では、「1. 速く 2. 訳さず英語のまま 3. なるべく辞書を使わず」に読むことが大切です。スピードを計るなど、速く読むよう心がけましょう（たとえば TOEIC® テストの音声スピードはおよそ1分間に150語です）。そして1語ずつ訳すのではなく、英語を英語のまま理解するくせをつけるようにします。こうして読み続けるうちに語感がついてきて、だんだんと英語が理解できるようになるのです。まずは、ラダーシリーズの中からあなたのレベルに合った本を選び、少しずつ英文に慣れ親しんでください。たくさんの本を手にとるうちに、英文書がすらすら読めるようになってくるはずです。

《本シリーズの特徴》
- 中学校レベルから中級者レベルまで5段階に分かれています。自分に合ったレベルからスタートしてください。
- クラシックから現代文学、ノンフィクション、ビジネスと幅広いジャンルを扱っています。あなたの興味に合わせてタイトルを選べます。
- 巻末のワードリストで、いつでもどこでも単語の意味を確認できます。レベル1、2では、文中の全ての単語が、レベル3以上は中学校レベル外の単語が掲載されています。
- カバーにヘッドホーンマークのついているタイトルは、オーディオ・サポートがあります。ウェブから購入／ダウンロードし、リスニング教材としても併用できます。

《使用語彙について》
レベル1：中学校で学習する単語約1000語
レベル2：レベル1の単語＋使用頻度の高い単語約300語
レベル3：レベル1の単語＋使用頻度の高い単語約600語
レベル4：レベル1の単語＋使用頻度の高い単語約1000語
レベル5：語彙制限なし

❦ Contents ❧

PROLOGUE		3
1	Is It the Ghost?	6
2	The New Margarita	12
3	The Rule Book	18
4	Box Five	24
5	In Perros	30
6	*Faust* and What Followed	37
7	The Masked Ball	42
8	Above the Trap-Doors	48
9	Erik	51
10	Christine! Christine!	60
11	Down into the Cellars	65
12	Inside the Torture Room	70
13	The Scorpion and the Grasshopper	80
14	The End of the Ghost's Love	85
Word List		94

読みはじめる前に

本書で使われている用語です。わからない語は巻末のワードリストで確認しましょう。

- [ ] ball
- [ ] blame
- [ ] box
- [ ] cellar
- [ ] dearly
- [ ] faint
- [ ] fit
- [ ] fame
- [ ] greet
- [ ] hatred
- [ ] kidnapping
- [ ] viscount

用語解説

Paris Opera House　パリ・オペラ座。パリに実在する歌劇場ガルニエ宮をモデルにしている

Faust　『ファウスト』　シャルル・グノーが作曲した全5幕のオペラ。ドイツの文豪ゲーテの劇詩『ファウスト』を題材にしている

Margarita　マルグリート《『ファウスト』のヒロイン》

foyer de ballet　バレリーナ共同控え室

set piece　大道具

Roi de Lahore　『ラホールの王』　ジュール・マスネが作曲したオペラ

主な登場人物

Opera Ghost　オペラ座の怪人：パリのオペラ座に住みついていると噂される謎の怪人

Christine Daae　クリスティーヌ・ダーエ：オペラ座の若手女優、ソプラノ歌手

Raoul de Chagny　ラウル・ド・シャニー：子爵、子供の頃にクリスティーヌと知り合い恋に落ちる

Philippe de Chagny　フィリップ・ド・シャニー：伯爵、弟のラウルを息子のように大切にしている

the Persian　ペルシャ人：謎の人物、オペラ座の怪人の秘密を知っている

Mr. Debienne　ドビエンヌ氏：オペラ座の前支配人

Mr. Poligny　ポリニー氏：オペラ座の前支配人

Sorelli　ソレリ：プリマ・バレリーナ

Cecile Jammes　セシル・ジャンム：若いバレリーナ

Joseph Buquet　ジョゼフ・ビュケ：道具方主任

Meg Giry　メグ・ジリー：若いバレリーナ

Carlotta　カルロッタ：ソプラノ歌手、オペラ座のスター

Mr. Moncharmin　モンシャルマン氏：オペラ座の新支配人

Mr. Richard　リシェール氏：オペラ座の新支配人

Mrs. Giry　ジリー夫人：ボックス席の案内係、メグの母親

Darius　ダリウス：「ペルシャ人」の召使い

The Phantom of the Opera

by Gaston Leroux

PROLOGUE

The opera ghost really existed. He was not just a story created by the actors, singers, and managers, or something imagined by the little dancers. He physically existed in flesh and blood, although he appeared to people as a ghost.

The story I have to tell deals with one of the saddest and most unbelievable events ever to take place at the Paris Opera House. It happened only about thirty years ago. In fact, if you visit the opera today, try asking some of the oldest men there about it. They will surely remember that event and tell you what they know.

That sad event, of course, is the kidnapping of Christine Daae, the sudden disappearance of Viscount Raoul de Chagny, and the death of his older brother, Count Philippe de Chagny, whose body was found on the shore of the underground lake that exists under the opera house.

When I began studying this terrible story at the National Academy of Music, I was surprised by how many connections there seemed to be between the "ghost" and the disappearance of these three people. Nobody who was there at the time seemed to think the ghost had anything to do with the disappearance of Christine Daae. But I slowly began to think that somehow the ghost was responsible for the terrible event.

I discovered that my beliefs were correct when I talked with the man known throughout Paris simply as "the Persian." The man had been there and witnessed some parts of the event. Greatly excited, I listened to his story. When he finished, he handed me evidence that the

PROLOGUE

ghost existed, including the strange letters of Christine Daae. Finally I could not doubt the story anymore. The ghost was real!

Is It the Ghost?

We'll begin our story on the evening that Mr. Debienne and Mr. Poligny, the managers of the opera, were throwing their retirement party. La Sorelli, one of the main dancers, was in her dressing room going over the speech she was to give for the two retiring managers. Suddenly, her door opened and a group of young dancers rushed into the room.

"It's the ghost!" cried little Jammes, one of the ballet girls. She locked the door.

Sorelli believed in ghosts. Little Jammes's words made her hands shake, but she tried to look calm.

Is It the Ghost?

"Have you seen him?" asked Sorelli.

"Yes! As plainly as I see you now!" said Jammes.

"He is very ugly!" added another dancer.

The dancers described what they had seen: a gentleman in dress clothes who suddenly appeared before them in the hall. He seemed to have come straight through a wall.

For several months now, all anybody at the opera had talked about was this ghost in dress clothes who appeared in different parts of the building. He spoke to nobody and disappeared as soon as he was seen. He made no noise when walking.

At first people laughed at the stories, but the ghost's fame grew and grew. Finally, any accident or strange event was blamed on the ghost. Every fall, every broken object, and every ballet shoe that went missing was thought to be the work of the opera ghost.

The girls all said the ghost was a skeleton with a death's head. This description had actually come from Joseph Buquet, the head scene-changer. He had *really* seen the ghost, unlike many of the ballet girls who often talked about the ghost but hadn't actually seen him. Joseph had seen him on a narrow, dark staircase that led down to the cellars of the opera.

"He is terribly thin, and his clothes hang on him as if on a skeleton," Joseph said. "His eyes are so deep they look like two black holes, just like in a dead man's skull. He has no nose. He has no hair either, except for three long, dark locks behind his ears!"

But let us return to the evening we were discussing.

"Listen!" said little Jammes as she put her ear to the door. Everyone fell silent, and they all listened hard. There was a slight sound outside—was it the sound of footsteps? Then it stopped, and there was only silence.

Sorelli, trying to look calm, went to the door and called out, "Who's there?"

There was no reply.

Sorelli suddenly opened the door and cried out, "Who's there?"

There was only an empty, dark hall. She quickly shut the door and turned to the girls.

"Nobody's there," she said. Then, secretly, so no one would see, she made the sign of the cross with her right hand.

"But we saw him!" said Jammes. "And yesterday, Gabriel the song-master saw him too! Gabriel was so afraid that he jumped up from his chair and hit his head on a hat peg. Then, hurrying out of the room he tripped and fell down the stairs! It was all the ghost's doing, you see!"

Then little Giry spoke up.

"My mother says we shouldn't talk about such things," she said.

"Why not?" said the girls, crowding around her. "Why not?"

"I—I promised I wouldn't tell!"

But the girls kept crowding around her and promised to keep her secret, so little Giry told them all that she knew.

"The ghost has a private box!"

"A box! At the opera? Tell us more!" said the ballet girls.

"Yes, it's Box Five. You know, on the top level, next to the stage-box. My mother is in charge of it. And she says nobody has used that box for a whole month except the ghost. The managers' office has ordered that tickets to that box must never be sold."

The girls stared with wide eyes.

"The ghost comes to the box and my mother gives him his program, but she has never seen him. The truth is he can't be seen! Do you understand? He has no dress clothes or a death's head! So all this talk about a skeleton isn't true! And my mother says talking about it will bring us bad luck."

Just then, they heard heavy footsteps in the hall, and someone called out, "Cecile Jammes! Are you there?"

"It's mother!" said little Jammes. She opened the door, and a rather large woman rushed into the room and dropped herself onto the sofa.

"It's so terrible!" she cried out.

"What, mother? What's happened?"

"Joseph Buquet is dead! He was found hanging in the third-floor cellar!"

The girls cried out and they all started talking at once.

"It's the ghost!" someone said.

"I shall never be able to give my speech," said Sorelli, closing her eyes.

The truth is, no one ever knew how Joseph Buquet died. The examiner said Joseph had killed himself. However, there are details that remain a mystery. When the managers were notified of the death, they had workers go to the cellar to cut the body down. But when they arrived, the body had already been cut down and the rope had disappeared.

The New Margarita

That same evening, Count Philippe de Chagny had brought his younger brother, Raoul, to his private box at the opera. Raoul was a young sailor and he had just returned to Paris several weeks ago after sailing around the world. He was a rather shy young man, and he had very soft, pretty features. Count Philippe was twenty years older than Raoul and was very proud of him.

Ever since his return, Raoul had taken up a great love for the opera. Also, Philippe was rather close with La Sorelli, and he thought Raoul might like to be introduced to some of the other beauties of the opera.

That evening, Christine Daae had shocked everyone with her version of *Faust*. She was a good singer, but she was never *great*, so Christine had been given only the smaller parts in the opera. However, that night, La Carlotta, the opera's main star, had fallen ill. Someone had to take the part of Margarita, one of the most important parts in *Faust*. In a rush, the managers told Christine to do it. They hadn't expected much. So, you can imagine everybody's surprise when she made her entrance and sang like an angel. No one had ever heard anything like it. That night, Christine showed Paris a new kind of Margarita—a splendid, haunting Margarita.

Everyone was shocked. Had Christine been hiding her true voice all this time? If so, why? Had the managers known that Christine had such a voice? Is that why they had chosen her, who had never been very good, to take the role of Margarita at the last minute? It was odd, because it was well-known that Christine did not have a professor of music at the time. She often said that she wanted to practice alone. It was all a mystery.

At the end of her song, as everyone jumped up and cheered for Christine, she fainted on stage.

Philippe turned to his brother and saw Raoul was quite pale.

"She just fainted!" Raoul said. He looked like he was going to faint himself. "Let's go see her. She never sang like that before."

Before Philippe could stop him, Raoul was headed to the *foyer de ballet*, walking past all the ballet girls, and turning into the hall that led to the dressing room of Christine Daae. Philippe thought it was strange that Raoul knew the way.

A crowd of people had gathered around Christine's room. They had all been excited by Christine's performance, as well as her fainting fit. The doctor arrived at the same time as Raoul. Christine was lying unconscious on the sofa.

"Doctor," said Raoul with a concerned face, "shouldn't you clear all these people out of here?"

The doctor agreed, and everyone was told to leave the room except for Christine, her maid, Raoul, and the doctor. Raoul simply acted like he should be there and the doctor did not kick him out.

When Christine finally awoke, Raoul was right next to her.

"Excuse me, sir," she said in a whisper, "but who are you?"

At this, Raoul got on his knee, kissed her hand, and said, "I am the little boy who went into the sea to save your scarf!"

This was such a strange thing to say that Christine began to laugh and was joined by the doctor and her maid. Raoul turned red.

"Miss Daae," he said, "if you do not recognize me, then I would like to say something to you in private—something important."

"Perhaps later," said Christine, sitting up.

"Please, all of you, leave me. I need some peace."

Everyone, including the doctor, left the room. After Christine's door closed, Raoul stayed in the hall, waiting for her to come out so he might speak to her. But he soon heard voices come from inside her room!

"Christine, you must love me!" said a man's voice. It sounded clear, strong, and rather demanding.

"How can you say that?" said Christine. "I sing only for you!"

She sounded as though she were crying.

"Are you tired?" asked the voice, more gently now.

"Tired? Tonight I gave you my soul and now I am dead!" she said.

"Your soul is beautiful," said the man, "and I thank you. No king ever received so wonderful a gift. Tonight you made the angels weep."

Raoul heard nothing after that. He was filled with love for one person in that room and hatred for the other. As his anger grew stronger, he suddenly heard the door open. He rushed to hide in the shadow of the hall, and he saw Christine, alone, pass him. When she disappeared down the hall, Raoul jumped into Christine's room, ready to meet the man with the clear, strong voice.

"Who's there?" he cried out.

There was no sound. Raoul turned on the lamps. He searched everywhere—but there was no one in the room.

The Rule Book

During this time, the retiring managers, Mr. Debienne and Mr. Poligny, were talking and laughing with their party guests. Sorelli and the dancers had made it to the *foyer de ballet* where Sorelli was about to make her speech. Nobody at the party yet knew about Joseph Buquet's death except for the ballet girls.

However, just as Sorelli had put on her famous smile, lifted her wine glass, and started to speak, her speech was cut short by little Jammes.

"The opera ghost!" cried out Jammes. She pointed toward the back of the crowd. But by the time the guests turned around to see who was there, the ghost had slipped away. He was gone.

The guests started laughing, believing it was a joke.

"The opera ghost!" they said as they pointed to their friends.

Sorelli, of course, was angry. She did not get to finish her speech, but the retiring managers thanked her and kissed her, then hurried up the stairs to the *foyer* of the singers. The singers and musicians were gathered there to make a speech for the managers also. After this was done, finally, on the third floor, the managers met their own guests and friends, who were gathered to make their speeches and to have dinner together.

It was here, on the third floor, that the old managers met the new managers, Mr. Moncharmin and Mr. Richard. They greeted the men who were to take over the opera the next day. The crowd around them settled into talk and laughter. It was during these pleasant moments when a few people began to notice a very thin, very ugly man sitting at the dinner table by himself.

The man had deep-set eyes, so deep that they looked like two black holes in his head. His dress clothes hung on him as though he were a skeleton. He was terrible to look at, but most people simply turned away and politely said nothing. So it was the opera ghost himself who spoke first.

"The death of Joseph Buquet is perhaps not a natural death," he said.

All talk in the room stopped.

"Is Buquet dead?" the old managers cried out.

"Yes," said the ghost. "He was found hanging in the third-floor cellar, between a set piece and a scene from the *Roi de Lahore*."

The managers turned white. They asked the new managers to join them in the manager's office. Once they had closed the door behind them, they asked the two new managers to sit, for they had a secret to tell them.

"Do you know who that man sitting at the table is?" Mr. Poligny asked Mr. Moncharmin and Mr. Richard. The new managers said no.

"That is the opera ghost," said Mr. Poligny. "He has ordered us to ask you, as the new managers, to give him anything he wants."

The new managers looked at each other and began laughing.

"What kind of joke is this?" asked Mr. Richard. But the old managers just stared at him, their faces like stone.

"This is not a joke," said Mr. Poligny. "Every time we do something that the ghost doesn't like, something terrible happens at the opera. The death of Joseph Buquet is the latest example."

"Well, what does the ghost want from us?" asked Mr. Richard. He tried to hide his smile, but he failed.

Mr. Poligny went to his desk and pulled out the rule book, which has been given to every manager since the start of the opera. The book stated that the manager of the opera would lose his job if he did not follow four rules. The rules were listed from one through four. At the end, a fifth rule had been written into the book by hand, in red ink, in very strange, child-like writing. It read:

"5. If the manager is late in paying the opera ghost the amount of twenty thousand francs a month, for a total of two hundred forty thousand francs a year, the manager shall be made to leave the opera."

"This was written by the ghost, you see?" said Mr. Debienne.

"Is this all?" asked Mr. Richard, who still believed this was all a very fine joke. "Doesn't he want anything else?"

"Yes," replied Mr. Poligny. He turned a few pages in the rule book and came to the part that listed the days in which certain private boxes must be made free for the president, the ministers, and so on. Here, again, a line had been added in red ink:

"Box Five on the top level shall be saved for the use of the opera ghost for every performance."

At this, the two new managers looked at each other and laughed out loud again.

"Very good, sirs, very good," they said, rising from their chairs. They shook the retiring managers' hands and left the room laughing.

"I see that we French are still excellent at creating jokes!" said Mr. Moncharmin. The two enjoyed the rest of the party without another thought about the opera ghost.

Box Five

Mr. Richard and Mr. Moncharmin enjoyed the first few days of being the new managers of the opera. They were very excited about working for such a famous institution. They forgot all about what the old managers had told them about the rule book and the ghost. Then, one morning, they received a letter that proved that the joke (if it was, indeed, a joke) was not over.

The letter was written in the same red ink and child-like writing as the lines added to the rule book. The letter read:

Box Five

Dear Mr. Manager,

I'm sorry to trouble you during this busy time. However, I had to bring to your attention something very important: I have found, on a few occasions, that my private box at the opera was filled by somebody else. I wrote to the old managers, Mr. Debienne and Mr. Poligny, to ask them to please explain. They replied by saying they had shown you the rule book and told you about my demands. So, I must assume that you are choosing not to respect my wishes.

Let me be clear: If you value your own safety, you must not take away my private box! I wish to see Christine Daae perform, and if I cannot do this from Box Five, you and other members of the opera will pay dearly.

Yours Truly,
Opera Ghost

When they were finished reading, the managers looked at each other. This joke seemed to be going too far. They decided to call in the box-keeper to their office to ask exactly what she knew about Box Five.

Mrs. Giry, the mother of the little dancer Meg Giry, soon came to the office. She was an older lady with gray hair and an old, black dress.

"How may I help you, sirs?" she asked.

"Mrs. Giry, you are the box-keeper, are you not? You know all the guests who own private boxes?"

"Yes, sir."

"Well, tell us about the guest who owns Box Five."

Mrs. Giry suddenly looked worried and didn't say anything.

"Well? What have you to say?" Mr. Richard demanded.

"I don't like to talk about Box Five, sir."

"Why not?"

"Because—because it's not good luck, sir. The owner of that box is the opera ghost."

"That's what I thought!" said Mr. Richard. "And who is this ghost exactly?"

"Why, I've never seen him! But I hear him. He thanks me when I put his program in the box."

"How is it that you don't see him but you do hear him?"

"Well ... He's a ghost, sir."

Mr. Richard was getting angry.

"Isn't there anything you can tell us that is of some use?" he cried out.

Mrs. Giry didn't like being talked to in this way. She stood up taller and put her nose in the air.

"I believe I've answered your questions to the best of my ability, sir," she said.

Mr. Moncharmin stepped in quickly.

"Dear Mrs. Giry," he said. "Don't mind Mr. Richard. He does not know how to speak to a lady." Here he threw an angry look at Mr. Richard.

"Please, if there is anything else you know about the guest who 'owns' Box Five, be so good as to tell us."

Mrs. Giry seemed to soften a bit.

"Well, I can tell you that the ghost likes to cause trouble when he doesn't get what he wants. For example, one night, when Mr. Poligny and Mr. Debienne were still quite new, they made the mistake of putting three guests in Box Five. It was Mr. and Mrs. Maniera—you know, they own that jewelry store in the center of town—and their friend, Mr. Isidore Saack. Well, when the show started, there was a great love scene. While the actors on stage were kissing, a voice whispered in Mr. Maniera's ear, 'Ha ha! Julie wouldn't mind giving a kiss to Isidore!' Mr. Maniera turned to his wife, Julie, and he saw that Mr. Saack was kissing her hand! Well, the two men started fighting! As Mr. Saack ran away, he fell down the grand staircase and broke his leg! It will be a long time before he can walk up those stairs again, I'm sure."

There was a quiet moment as the managers thought about this story.

"You have been very helpful, Mrs. Giry," said Mr. Moncharmin. "Thank you very much for your time. You are free to go."

When Mrs. Giry had left the room, the two managers turned to each other.

"I am not at all impressed," said Mr. Richard firmly. "That story doesn't prove anything about any ghost."

"Quite right," said Mr. Moncharmin. "Let's forget about this ghost! He is nothing but an old wives' tale."

With that, the managers went about their business.

In Perros

Meanwhile, Christine Daae did not give any more wonderful performances at the opera. She went back to being good but not *great*. She even turned down a few offers to perform at parties and shows. People tried to guess why she hid from attention. I believe the reason was fear. Christine was afraid of her own excellence, and she was afraid of what had happened to her that evening that she performed as Margarita.

She did not go out, and she didn't reply to any of Raoul's letters until one morning, she wrote him this note:

In Perros

Dear Sir,

I have not forgotten the little boy who went into the sea to save my scarf. I felt I had to write to you today, before I go to Perros. Tomorrow is the anniversary of my father's death. You knew my father, and he liked you very much. He is buried in Perros with his violin, by the little church. It is at the bottom of the hill where we used to play as children—the same place we said goodbye for the last time.

After reading this letter, Raoul caught the first train to Perros. As he traveled, he remembered the story of the little Swedish singer and her father.

There was once a poor man named Daae who had a little daughter, Christine. They lived in Sweden until Daae's wife passed away. Christine was still very young at the time. With no money or land, Daae brought Christine to the sea-side town of Perros, France, for a chance at a better life.

Many people believed Daae was the best violin player in all of France—some believed in all the world. His daughter also had the voice of an angel, and the two would stand together on the street and perform some of the most beautiful music anyone had ever heard.

One summer, a little boy who was to grow up to become the Viscount of Chagny came to Perros with his aunt. This boy was, of course, Raoul.

For young Raoul, it was love at first sight. He followed Christine and her father to the sea, where they went walking one afternoon. The wind was strong that day and blew Christine's scarf into the sea.

"Don't worry, Miss," said Raoul. "I'll get your scarf for you!"

He ran straight into the sea. When he returned the scarf to Christine, she was so happy that she kissed him. His aunt, meanwhile, was not very happy.

From that day, Christine and Raoul were

In Perros

great friends. They spent many hours playing together and listening to Daae's stories. Their favorite story was about the Angel of Music. Whoever the Angel of Music visited on earth would become a musical genius. Daae told Christine that he would send her the Angel of Music someday, once he had died and gone to heaven.

Finally, when Raoul had to leave Perros, he and Christine said goodbye at the bottom of the hill where they often played.

"I shall never forget you!" Raoul said.

Christine had tears in her eyes as he walked away. Raoul, too, felt like crying, for he knew that a poor girl like Christine could never be the wife of the Viscount of Chagny.

As the years passed, Christine often thought of Raoul and continued to sing. However, when her father died, she seemed to lose her voice. She sang well enough to get into music school, where she did not shine but did well enough to become a part of the Paris Opera. Raoul knew this and had come to see her perform when he returned to Paris. However, he was surprised to find that she did not sing as well as she once did. In fact, since her father's death, nobody heard the true quality of her voice until the night she sang as Margarita. That night, it was as if she was Christine Daae again, the girl with the voice that could make angels cry.

Suddenly, the train came to a stop. Raoul had arrived in Perros. He asked the workers at the station if they had seen a Parisian woman with long, golden hair. They told him that they saw a woman with hair like that go to the Setting Sun Inn that day. Raoul hurried there.

Raoul opened the door of the Setting Sun to find Christine sitting there. She was smiling and waiting for him.

"Hello, my old friend," she said. "I'm glad to see you here."

"Christine! Finally, you speak to me!" said Raoul. He rushed toward her and took her hands. Then, his feelings took over and Raoul spoke angrily.

"Why did you not reply to any of my letters? Why did you not recognize me before? Haven't you ever seen me at the opera? I even followed you to your room several times, but you acted like you never saw me!"

Christine turned red.

"Yes, I had seen you," she said.

"Why did you never speak to me? Don't you know that I love you?"

"Please, don't be foolish," said Christine, turning away. "You can't love a poor opera girl like me."

"Do you love someone else?" demanded Raoul. "I heard a man's voice in your room that night! That night you fainted," he said.

Suddenly, Christine looked at him with fear.

"Whose voice?" she demanded.

"The man who said, 'You must love me, Christine!' Then you said you had given your soul to him! He replied, 'Your soul is a beautiful thing.'"

Christine put a hand over her heart. She sat down and was still for a long time. Finally, she looked at Raoul.

"I ... I have a secret," she said. "Do you remember my father telling me that he would send me the Angel of Music after he died? Well, he has died, and he has sent him to me!"

"What do you mean?"

"That voice you heard in my room that night—it's him. The Angel of Music comes to me in my dressing room every day. I never see him, but I can hear him. I didn't know anyone else could hear him, but you heard him too!"

"If you're joking, stop this. I don't like it," said Raoul.

"I'm telling the truth, Raoul!" said Christine. "The Angel of Music teaches me how to sing, and he says I will become the greatest singer in the world!"

Faust and What Followed

In the following weeks, the managers of the opera sold tickets to Box Five with no regard to the threats of the opera ghost. They decided to end the whole idea of the ghost once and for all. They let everybody know that on Saturday evening, when *Faust* was to be performed, the managers themselves would sit in Box Five to watch the show.

But, on Saturday, as the managers settled into their seats, they seemed worried. They looked at each other, not quite knowing what to expect. However, as the first act ended without any problems, they began to feel relief. They even started joking to each other, saying, "Has anybody whispered in your ear yet?"

The second act also came and went with no problems. The managers were quite happy now and laughed quietly to themselves as they watched the show.

Carlotta made her entrance as Margarita and sang her first few lines. The rest of the act went beautifully. After the act ended, there was a short intermission, and the managers went out of the private box to talk for a few minutes. When they returned to their seats, they found a box of chocolates there.

"That's strange," said Mr. Moncharmin. "Who could have brought those in here?"

They settled back into their seats to watch the rest of the show. Also watching just a few boxes down were Raoul and Philippe de Chagny. They had come to see Christine Daae, who was playing the part of Siebel in *Faust*. However, Christine's singing was off that night, and she was causing more than one person in the audience to whisper, "What is wrong with that girl? One night she sings like an angel, and the next night she sounds like some singer off the street!"

Philippe was angry—he had written to the managers of the opera to praise Christine. Knowing that his brother, Raoul, loved Christine, he had hoped to advance her position at the opera. He had put his good name on the line for her, yet this is how she performed? How dare she!

Raoul, on the other hand, was quietly crying. He could not bear to watch Christine. She had lost all her cheer, all her vivacity! It made him sad—sadder than the letter he had received from her the day before. It had read:

My dear friend,

You and I must never see each other any more. If you truly love me, please do this for me. My life and your life depend on it.

Your Christine

Now, on the stage, Carlotta was singing her finest. She was getting to the most beautiful part of Margarita's song. As she threw back her shoulders and smiled wide for the crowd, she opened her mouth and this is the sound that came out:

"Co-ack!"

There was a moment of shock. Carlotta blinked a couple of times in wonder, then shook off the strange event. She opened her mouth, and again she sang, "Co-ack!"

The audience went wild.

"What kind of show is this? Is she sick? What's happened?"

Carlotta tried again and again to control her voice, but she only sang, "Co-ack! Co-ack! Co-ack!"

It was hopeless. Her voice had gone, and Carlotta stood on the stage in total shock. The guests filling the opera house cried out in anger. Surely, this was not what they had paid good money to see!

In Box Five, the managers turned white and closed their eyes. The opera ghost had struck! He was laughing at them! Then, very clearly, they heard a voice close to them say, "She is singing tonight to bring down the chandelier!" Then Box Five filled with his laughter.

Suddenly, the managers looked to the ceiling where the huge glass chandelier was hanging. In a moment, before anyone could do anything, the chandelier came crashing down to the floor below. As people ran, the voice kept laughing.

The newspaper the next day reported that many had been hurt and one person had been killed by the chandelier. People reading the newspaper thought to themselves, "The opera must be cursed."

The Masked Ball

That terrible event was bad for everyone. Carlotta fell ill. Christine disappeared. She was not seen or heard of for ten days after the performance. Then, one morning, as Raoul sat in his bedroom lost in sad thoughts, his servant brought him a letter.

Raoul recognized the paper and writing. He tore open the letter and read,

My dear Raoul,

Go to the masked ball at the opera tomorrow night. At twelve o'clock, be in the little room

THE MASKED BALL

behind the grand staircase and stand by the door. Wear a white cape and mask. Do not let yourself be recognized.

Christine

Raoul wondered what all this was about, and he was getting quite tired of such strange letters. Christine seemed strange all the time—first acting as if she didn't know him, then telling him to come to Perros. Then she had told him that story of the Angel of Music coming to her dressing room. Raoul did not know what to make of that. It was all too strange, but his heart called out for Christine. That day, he bought a white cape and mask. The next night, Raoul went to the ball.

The opera was filled with people. Making his way through the guests, Raoul found the little room behind the grand staircase. Although the room was crowded, by twelve, he had found some space to stand by the door. Suddenly, a woman in a black cape and mask came toward him and touched his arm. She walked out the door without a word and Raoul followed. It was Christine!

As they made their way through the ball, Raoul didn't even notice the wonderful dress clothes of the guests. However, there was one man he did notice: He was dressed all in red, with a long, red cape that dragged on the ground behind him. He walked proudly like a king, but his face was a perfect death's head! His eyes, nose, and mouth were four black holes. On his cape were the gold words, "Do not touch me! I am Red Death walking!"

Everybody was very impressed with Red Death. Some skilled artist must have created that wonderful death's head! Some guests even followed Red Death around. But Raoul noticed as they moved through the opera that Red Death seemed to be following him and Christine.

Raoul followed Christine up the stairs to a

private box. She kept looking over her shoulder. Before she shut the door of the private box behind them, she heard footsteps on the stairs. Quickly she looked out the door and saw a red foot on a stair, then a red leg—

"It is he!" she whispered and shut the door.

"Is that the man who you sing for and you give your soul to?" said Raoul. "That man dressed as Red Death is your Angel of Music? Well, I have something to say to him. I'll tear off his mask and tear off my own, and we'll speak to each other honestly, like men, and see who really loves you!"

Raoul tried to open the door but Christine blocked his way.

"You must not!" she cried. "Please, my love, please do not go out there!"

Raoul suddenly stopped.

"Christine," he said, "did you say 'my love'?"

It was the first time he had heard her say that she loved him.

"Yes, dear," she said. "And if you love me too,

you must never be seen or recognized by *him*."

She reached out her hands to Raoul, and he noticed she was wearing a gold ring on her finger.

"Christine!" cried Raoul. "Did *he* give you that? How can you tell me you love me, but wear his ring?"

Christine's hands dropped.

"I have to," she said sadly, "or terrible things will happen. You will never understand *his* sadness, or mine. He will hurt people, including you, if I do not go live with him."

She removed her mask, and Raoul saw the deep sadness on her face.

"Christine!" he cried. "What do you mean you have to live with him? What have you done?"

"My love," she said, "please, let us be happy together for this one month. I know you will leave Paris to go sailing again in four weeks. Before you go away, can we be secretly engaged? *He* will be working for the next month. But when he is done working, he will come for me.

Our month of happiness will be over ... but it will have been the best time of my life!"

Raoul got on one knee in front of her. He hardly knew what he was doing, and he didn't understand everything she was saying, but there was nothing more he wanted than to be married to this singer whom he had loved all his life.

"Christine," he said, "may I have your hand in marriage?"

She put her hand into his and said happily, "You already have it!"

Above the Trap-Doors

So began Christine and Raoul's month of happiness. She called for him to come to her dressing room most nights at the opera. On days they did not see each other, they wrote letters. This was also the high point of Christine's career as a singer. Angry about her terrible performance, Carlotta had canceled her contract and Christine had taken her place. After signing the contract, Christine had disappeared for two whole days, but when she came back, she sang like never before. She won over everyone at every performance. It was as if some angel had touched her and given her a voice from heaven.

Above the Trap-Doors

Raoul was filled with joy every time he visited Christine in her dressing room. One day, however, she did not notice he was at her door. Raoul saw her looking sadly into her mirror and saying softly, "Poor Erik ... Poor Erik."

Raoul felt a rush of anger—he was sure this was the name of Christine's Angel of Music.

"But I'll show her how happy we are together," thought Raoul, "and make her forget all about this 'Erik.' He won't take her from me again!" With that, he walked into her room with a smile, as if he had seen and heard nothing.

Christine and Raoul often walked throughout the opera—all seventeen floors of it, behind, over, and under the stage, in all the hidden corners and secret halls. One day, Raoul saw an open trap-door in the floor and looked down into the darkness below.

"You've taken me all through the opera, Christine, but you've never taken me to the world below. I know there are many cellars. Shall we go?"

But, shaking and with her eyes wide with fear, Christine pulled him away from the trap-door and said, "No! No! Everything underground belongs to *him*!"

When she said this, the trap-door suddenly shut. She pulled Raoul away, saying there were much nicer things to see on top of the roof, in the sun and among the birds. As she led him away, she looked over her shoulder. However, she didn't see the shadow that followed her.

Erik

Christine led Raoul to the roof, and there they saw all of Paris below them. It was just around sunset, and they sat down together for a while. But soon, Christine started to shake and seemed very worried.

"What is it, my love?" asked Raoul gently.

"Dear, I feel I must tell you everything. Here, on the roof, we are as far away from *him* as we can be. Our time together is running out, and before we part, I must let you know the truth."

Then, Christine began to tell her story.

"I called him 'the voice' before I knew his name was Erik," she said. "About three months ago, when I was in my dressing room, I heard a beautiful voice. It was singing, and I had never heard anything like it. I looked out into the hall and in all the rooms near mine, but nobody was there. So I had a foolish idea.

"My father told me he would send me the Angel of Music when he died. Well, my poor father died, and I waited, but the angel never came. So I called out to the voice, 'Are you my Angel of Music whom my father has sent to me?'

"'Yes!' it replied.

"Since then, the voice and I became great friends. We talked every day. Then the voice asked if it could give me music lessons. I said yes. The voice taught me so many wonderful things, and I found that I could sing like never before. But I kept it a secret because the voice, my teacher, told me it was not time to show the world yet.

"One day, I recognized you, dear, at the opera. You must have just returned to Paris from your travels. I was so happy to see you that I told the voice about you. But the voice became quiet. I called out to it again and again but it didn't reply. I was afraid it had gone forever.

"The next night, the voice came back. I was so happy it had not left me! It said I was ready to let the world hear the music of heaven. That night, Carlotta fell ill and I gave my best performance. I sang so hard it was as if my soul were leaving me. It was beautiful, but I was also afraid of it all! I fainted, and when I woke, I saw you.

"I knew the voice was there, so I acted like I didn't recognize you. Even so, the voice continued to be jealous, saying bad things about you every day. I got tired of it and I told the voice, 'That's enough. I'm going to Perros tomorrow and I'm going to ask Raoul to come with me.' The voice said that was fine, but if I married anyone on earth, he would leave me forever.

"Then, on the night that the chandelier fell, I was so afraid for you and the voice. I knew you were safe because I saw you in your brother's box. I thought if the voice was safe too, he would probably be in my dressing room. I ran there and called out to the voice. Suddenly, I can't explain how, but I heard the voice singing and my mirrors doubled and opened. When I walked toward it, I was suddenly outside of my room!

"It was dark and cold. The singing had stopped. A man in a black cape appeared and held me tightly. I struggled, but he put his hand over my mouth. His hand smelled like death! I fainted, and when I awoke, I was in a boat on an underground lake. The man with the black cape was taking me somewhere. He wore a mask that covered his whole face.

"We finally came to a bright place. It was a house on the edge of the lake! The man finally spoke. He said, 'Don't worry Christine, you're safe here.' It was the voice!

"I was angry and I cried out, 'Why have you brought me here? What do you want with me?' The voice just said, 'Come, I have something to show you.' He must have given me some drug because I followed.

"First, he showed me a lovely bedroom. He said this was where I would stay. Then he showed me his bedroom ... Oh, it was terrible! The walls were all black, with music notes written all over them. A huge organ covered one entire wall. And his bed ... his bed was a coffin!

"I was very afraid. 'Who are you?' I asked. He took me into a living room then, and he sat me down. Then, he fell at my feet and told me he was sorry!

"'I'm sorry, Christine,' he said. 'I lied. I'm not your Angel of Music. I'm not even a ghost. I'm just a man, and my name is Erik. This is where I live, Christine, and I love you! I want you to stay with me!'

"I suppose you will be angry with me, Raoul, but in that moment I pitied him. A man, living all alone under the opera, and with such a beautiful voice that no one knows about—how sad and lonely his life must be!

"I asked him to take off his mask, but he refused. Then, when he wasn't expecting it, I reached out and pulled his mask away! Oh! It was horrible, Raoul, horrible!"

"What, Christine? What did you see?"

"Erik is a living dead man! He has a death's head—his eyes, nose, and mouth are four large black holes! He was so angry that I saw his face that he grabbed me by my hair and pulled me into my room—"

"Enough!" cried Raoul, his heart in pain.

"—and he ran into his room, shut the door, and began to play the organ. The song was beautiful and frightening at the same time! It made everything at the opera seem like child's play. It expressed every human emotion possible. I later found out it is called *Don Juan Triumphant*. It is Erik's masterpiece.

"I was afraid, but the music took hold of me. I rose and slowly walked to his room. I opened the door and watched him play. He was crying. I said to him, 'Erik! Show me your face without fear!

Erik

You are the most unhappy of men, but you are a genius of music! If I ever look at you and have to turn away, it is not because of your face. It is because I am thinking of your pure genius!'

"He slowly turned to me then, for he believed me. It was a terrible sight—a skull crying. But I went to him, and I touched his arm. He stopped playing and he fell at my feet with words of love.

"And so it went, for the next ten days. We sang together almost all the time. The music was the most beautiful I have ever heard, but of course I cannot love him! I acted like I was happy, and after the tenth day, he told me I could be free, as long as I came to visit him often. He gave me this gold ring, and showed me the way out of the underground house on the lake."

Christine put her arms around Raoul as she finished her story.

"We must run away tonight," Raoul said, holding her tightly. "We must leave Erik for good!"

"We cannot," she said simply. "Erik has let me

go, but only for now. A few days after I returned to the opera, Erik's voice came and spoke to me in my dressing room. He said he knew I loved you, but he also knew that you were going away in a month. He said he loved me so much he could not bear to be without me. He said I could spend a month together with you if I came to live with him afterward. He said he would spend this month working on *Don Juan Triumphant*, and when he was done, we would marry! If I didn't agree to this, he said, he would do terrible things to my friends!"

Christine looked into Raoul's eyes.

"You see? I cannot hate Erik, because I pity him. Nobody has ever loved him. But he is truly a monster, and I must do as he says!"

"No, Christine, he is not your master!" said Raoul. "I will help you leave him! You will live the life you want! You want to be with me, don't you?"

"Yes, I love you!" said Christine. "I would do anything to be with you. Yes, you're right!

Let's leave this place forever! But I can't leave now—it would kill him if I left now. Let him hear me sing tomorrow. After the performance, at midnight, you must come and take me away!" Christine grew excited and her eyes shone. "At midnight, you must take me away from here!"

The young lovers held each other close. They did not notice the shadow behind them, which had heard every word.

Christine! Christine!

The next day, Raoul secretly prepared to leave Paris with Christine. A horse and carriage, money, food, extra clothing, and hired help were all ready by nine o'clock at night. By then, it was time to go to the opera.

That night, the opera was showing *Faust*. Raoul settled into his private box with his brother, Count Philippe de Chagny.

The first act was splendid. Christine made her entrance in the second act, and her voice was more beautiful than ever. People felt like they were listening to the angels singing in heaven.

Then, at the most moving part of *Faust*,

Christine held out her arms and sang the words, "My spirit longs to be with you!"

Suddenly, the opera went totally dark. The music stopped. Then, just as suddenly, the lights came back on. But Christine Daae was not on the stage!

The singers and actors looked at each other in shock. Guests began to whisper to each other, "What is this? Surely this isn't part of the show?"

Suddenly, one by one, everyone in the opera realized that Christine had disappeared and she wasn't coming back!

The whole opera went wild. Raoul jumped from his seat and ran to his carriage waiting outside. The carriage was still there, but it was empty—no Christine! What had happened? Where had she gone? Had that monster Erik taken her?

Raoul looked all around him in a fit of madness.

"Christine!" he cried out. "Christine!"

It took a while for Raoul to calm down and think clearly. He finally realized the best thing to do was to go to the managers and see if they knew anything. At the managers' office, he was met by the police chief, who had rushed to the opera as soon as he learned that a singer had disappeared.

In the office, Raoul told the managers and the police chief the story of Erik, his underground house by the lake, and his terrible love for Christine.

"He has her, I know it! We must go under the opera, but how do we get there? Please, you must tell me how!"

Both managers looked at each other and the police chief just stared at Raoul. Nobody said anything.

"Well? Can you help me?" asked Raoul.

"Dear Viscount," the police chief finally said, "you were planning on running away with Christine after the show tonight, correct?"

"Yes, sir."

"And you had a carriage ready for this?"

"Yes, sir."

"And did you notice whose carriage had drawn up next to yours tonight?"

"No, sir.

"It was your brother's. And did you notice that his carriage is now gone?"

"No, sir."

"I believe that your brother has taken Christine with him. Perhaps he didn't agree to your marriage. Perhaps he loved her too! Either way, Christine is gone, and so is your brother, Count Philippe de Chagny."

"Philippe!" cried out Raoul. "I will find him!"

He jumped up and ran out the door. His mind was racing, and again, he was not thinking clearly. But as soon as he began to run down the hall, he was stopped by a strange man. He had dark skin and green eyes that shone. Raoul had seen him at the opera before. He tried to think who it was ... It was the Persian!

"Viscount of Chagny," said the Persian, "I

know the monster named Erik. I believe he has taken Christine, and I think I can help you save her!"

Down into the Cellars

"I know Erik well," said the Persian. "I feel partly responsible for what he has done. I feel that I should have let him die when I had the chance! Then he would never have caused so much trouble, death, and pain! But we don't have much time. You must follow me and do everything I say. Our lives depend on it."

Raoul studied the Persian. He was a tall man in dress clothes, and he wore a Persian hat. He looked like he was telling the truth. Besides, this was the only other person who knew about Erik! Raoul decided to follow him, and they hurried down the hall. They came to Christine's dressing room.

"In here," said the Persian. When they entered, the Persian knocked softly three times on the wall. Suddenly, a hidden door in the wall opened, and a short man also wearing a Persian hat entered. He put two guns on the table.

"This is my servant, Darius," the Persian explained to Raoul. "He knows the opera as well as I do. I sent for him and these guns as soon as I heard Christine went missing." The Persian turned to the man.

"Were you followed?" he asked. The man shook his head no.

"Thank you, Darius. You may go."

Darius left through the same hidden door. Raoul watched all this with surprise.

As the Persian checked the guns, he explained, "That door is one of the ways Erik gets into Christine's room. The other way is this."

He reached up to a corner of the wall near the ceiling. He pushed something there, and suddenly, the mirror doubled and opened up!

"Erik built all these things. Back in my country, Erik was called 'the trap-door lover.' Here, in Paris, he was one of the chief builders of this opera house."

All this information was creating more questions in Raoul's mind than answers. But there was no time for talking.

"Here, take this gun. Be very quiet, and follow me!" said the Persian.

With that, the two men stepped through the mirror into a cold, dark hall.

"Before we go," said the Persian, "you must hold your gun out in front of you, as if you are about to shoot. Hold your whole arm out, and keep your hand at the same height as your eyes. Always hold your arm out like this! Now, let's go!"

Holding his gun in front of him, the Persian led the way deeper into the darkness.

They made their way through the cellars for what seemed to be a long time. Raoul was surprised at how well the Persian knew the opera house. The Persian was, perhaps, the best guide he could have asked for.

Most of the time they were able to walk, but sometimes they had to crawl through small spaces. No matter what, they always held their arms out as if they were about to shoot. When Raoul said that his arm was getting tired holding the gun this way, the Persian told him to put the gun in his pocket but to keep his arm out in front of him.

"But how could that possibly help?" asked Raoul.

The Persian turned around to face him. He was very serious.

"I don't have enough time to explain everything," he said, "but I will tell you this much: Erik lived for some time in India. While he was there, he became very skilled at using rope. In fact, he became a master strangler. For a while, he earned money by fighting soldiers and strong men with only a rope. Just when the soldier, armed with a sword, thought he would win,

Erik would throw the rope perfectly around the soldier's neck and pull the rope tight until he died. This is why you must hold your arm out. Erik could be looking for us, waiting for us, or following us. He won't be able to throw the rope around your neck if you're in this position. It is a matter of life or death."

The Persian then continued on his way. Raoul followed without asking any more questions.

Inside the Torture Room

Finally, they arrived in the third cellar, where Joseph Buquet was found hanging. The Persian knew this area was the back entrance to Erik's house because he had started to follow Erik several weeks ago. Once the Persian knew Erik was in love with Christine, he began to worry for her safety. He secretly followed Erik around to understand where he went, how he entered his house, and where he might end up taking Christine. One day, the Persian had followed Erik to this spot, where he had seen him remove a large stone from a wall. Erik had climbed into his house through the hole in the wall, and the

Persian knew this was where they could enter.

"This is the back of Erik's house," whispered the Persian. "I believe it's safer to enter through here than the front, by the lake. Once we enter, we must not talk at all, for Erik might hear us."

The Persian reached up and carefully removed a large stone from the wall.

"Take off your shoes," he mouthed to Raoul. Then, he climbed up and in through the hole, disappearing into Erik's house. Raoul followed.

When Raoul quietly dropped to the ground, he saw something that shocked him. Although it was quite dark, he could see that they were in a forest. Many men were there with them! The Persian saw Raoul's eyes open wide with surprise, and he took hold of the young man's arm. The Persian walked towards one of the trees and put Raoul's hand on it. It was cold—how strange! It was made of iron. Then the Persian walked towards one of the men, who also started walking toward him! The Persian put his hand out, and the man also put his hand out. Their hands touched. Raoul finally realized what was happening. It was a mirror! All the walls were mirrors!

Looking carefully, Raoul could see that there was only one iron tree in the room, and they were the only men. He could also see the edges of the mirrors where they met. He counted six mirrors. So they had dropped into a small, six-sided room made entirely of mirrors. What kind of place was this?

The Persian looked all around him and knew that they had entered a terrible place. In Persia, he had seen Erik build a room like this for the king. It was a torture room. The Persian looked at the iron tree and saw something that filled him with fear. A rope hung from a branch. The Persian thought of Joseph Buquet. Perhaps this was the rope from which he had hung.

Suddenly, the two men heard footsteps in a room nearby. Then they heard a voice.

"I love you, Christine. But you do not love me!"

It was Erik! Then, they heard Christine crying. She was alive!

"I will give you a choice," said Erik. "You have until eleven o'clock tomorrow to decide: Will we play the wedding song or the song for the dead? The wedding song is very lovely, Christine. The song for the dead is not quite as nice. You must decide either to marry me or die with me!"

Christine said nothing, though she continued to cry.

"I know what will help you decide, my love. If you do not choose to marry me, we will not be the only ones to die. *Everyone* will die! I have a plan, you see. If we do not marry at eleven o'clock tomorrow night, everyone will be dead!"

The Persian became very concerned. What did Erik mean? How would everyone die? What was his plan?

Just then, there was a loud ringing sound, like an alarm clock.

"A visitor at the lake!" cried Erik angrily. "Who could have come down here? I must go tell this visitor he is not wanted!" He rushed across the room and they all heard a door open and close behind him.

This was Raoul's chance. He called out, "Christine! Christine! It is Raoul! We will save you!"

Christine called back, "Raoul? Can it really be you? Oh, you must run! Run far away from this place!"

"Christine," the Persian cut in, "I am here to help Raoul. But we are trapped in a room with no door. All the walls in here are mirrors. I believe it is the torture room. Can you get us out of here?"

"I can't!" cried out Christine. "I'm tied up!"

"That monster!" said Raoul. "Why has he tied you?"

"I tried to kill myself. When he brought me down here, I tried to kill myself by hitting my head against the wall. He tied me up, for I am not allowed to die until eleven o'clock tomorrow."

"No!" cried Raoul.

"Never mind," said the Persian. He knew they had to act quickly. He called out to Christine, "Listen to me, my dear. Do you know where the door to the torture room is?"

"No," she replied. "But I know where he keeps the keys!"

"Good! Now listen closely. Erik loves you. Because of this, you have power over him. Be sweet to him and tell him what he wants to hear. Then have him untie you. If you are free to move, my dear, you can get the key, and we will figure out how to get out of here safely!"

Suddenly, they heard the monster enter again.

"I'm back, my love," he said to Christine. "I'm sorry I had to go, but we don't want any visitors, do we? Don't worry, I took care of him. He won't ever visit again."

Both Raoul and the Persian wondered who the poor visitor was. Who would know to come down here, to the house by the lake? Whoever he was, what had happened to him?

Then Christine spoke softly.

"No, I don't care for visitors when you are with me, Erik."

Yes, thought the Persian. That's right, Christine! Be sweet and use your power over him!

"Erik, dear, can you please untie me? These ropes are hurting me."

"Oh, my love! Have I hurt you? I am so sorry ... Is that better?"

"Yes, much better. Thank you."

"I know what will make you feel better, my love. Music! You shall hear me play the song for the dead for our little visitor!"

Raoul and the Persian's hearts turned cold. So the visitor must be dead! They heard Erik run into another room and begin to play the organ. He played beautifully. But suddenly he stopped and cried out, "Where is my bag with the keys?"

There were loud footsteps, and soon the two men heard Christine cry out in pain.

She must have taken the keys, thought the

Inside the Torture Room

Persian, and he must have hurt her to get them back.

"Aha!" cried Erik. "Why are you stealing from me? You mustn't ever steal from Erik!"

Again, Christine cried out in pain.

Raoul, unable to control himself, cried out, "Leave her alone!"

"What?" said Erik. "There is someone here! Christine, you know there is someone here and you are trying to help him! You are trying to run away! Well, I won't let you! And I shall teach your friend a lesson he won't forget!"

They heard Erik's footsteps come toward the torture room. It sounded like he was climbing some stairs, and then they heard the sound of a curtain being pushed aside. A little light suddenly came into the torture room. Raoul and the Persian looked up, and there, near the ceiling, was a narrow window, just big enough for a pair of eyes to look through. They saw two eyes like black holes, angry eyes, looking down at them.

"Your friends are hiding in the torture room,"

said Erik. "Well, let's give them a *warm* welcome. I believe they will be feeling quite warm soon!"

Suddenly, very bright, very hot lights turned on in the torture room. Raoul and the Persian started to sweat.

"These lights!" cried Raoul. "They are so bright and hot—it feels like we will burn alive!"

"Raoul, we must stay calm," said the Persian. "The heat will make us lose our minds if we are not careful. This is how Erik tortures people. Once you decide you cannot take any more heat, it is very easy to tell yourself to use the rope on that tree! You must stay calm. I know Erik well, so I will look for the hidden button that will open the door to let us out of here."

Raoul was silent. The Persian got to work looking for the hidden button. He felt and studied every inch of each mirror carefully. He was done with three, with only three left to go, when Raoul began to talk of water.

"I must drink … I don't know how much longer I can take this … "

"Raoul!" said the Persian, going to him, "You must stay strong! Do not think of water. Don't worry, I will find the button soon."

But when the Persian turned back to the mirrors, he wasn't sure which he had already studied and which were left. He had to begin all over again!

Neither of them knew how much time had passed. Raoul lay on the ground. He couldn't speak in full sentences.

"Christine ... The monster won't let us out ... Water ... "

By this time, the Persian was not doing much better. He could not see straight, and his legs gave out. He fell to the floor. Under the bright lights, both men closed their eyes and slipped into darkness.

The Scorpion and the Grasshopper

The Persian did not know how long he had been lying there when he awoke. As his vision came back to him, he saw a small black nail sticking out of the floor near the iron tree.

His eyes opened wide and he quickly sat up.

"Raoul! Wake up! I've found it!"

He knew this had to be the button to the door.

Raoul sat up with some difficulty. The Persian reached out and pressed the button.

A trap-door in the floor opened down into a dark staircase.

"Come, Raoul!"

They went down into the dark, feeling the cool air on their hot faces. They smiled like children and continued to go down. Soon they came to a room full of barrels.

"Perhaps it's water! Or wine!" cried Raoul.

Both men quickly took a barrel and opened it. But what they found was not water or wine—it was gun powder!

The Persian went cold with fear. He now knew Erik's plan. If Christine didn't marry him, he was going to blow up the Paris Opera House! The arranged time of eleven o'clock now made sense to him: it was the time the opera was filled with people watching a show.

"What time is it?" cried the Persian. "How long have we been here? It may be too late!"

They ran up the steps to the torture room, but the light was now turned off. Erik must have realized they had escaped. Suddenly, they heard Christine's voice.

"Raoul! Raoul!"

"Christine! Are you safe? There's gun powder

here, Christine! He means to blow up the whole opera house! We must stop him, Christine! What time is it?"

"It is five minutes to eleven!" she replied. "I must marry him, Raoul. Forgive me! I must marry him or everyone will die! He has left to prepare some final things. He said there are two boxes here on the table. One holds a scorpion and the other a grasshopper. They are both made of iron. If I choose to marry him, I'm to turn the scorpion. If I choose death, I'm to turn the grasshopper."

"Wait!" cried the Persian. "You say they are made of iron and you must turn one?"

"Yes!"

"Don't touch either!" cried the Persian. "They are both devices! I'm sure the grasshopper is connected to something that will blow up the gun powder. I believe the scorpion is connected to something too, I just don't know what!"

Just then they all heard Erik's voice. He had returned, and he had heard them talking.

"Very good, my friend!" he said. "You are correct! But it is Christine's choice, and it is now eleven o'clock. You must choose, Christine. To marry me, turn the scorpion! To die, turn the grasshopper!"

Raoul and the Persian held their breath as they waited. Suddenly, they heard a sound—but it wasn't an explosion, it was the sound of water!

"Christine chooses the scorpion!" Erik cried. "Come! We must be married!"

"But what will happen with the scorpion?" cried out Christine.

"Turning it releases water from the lake to flow into the room holding the gun powder. All the powder will be washed away. You have saved everyone at the opera, my love. However, you must say goodbye to Raoul and his friend, for the water will fill the torture room too! Now, come!"

As Erik spoke, the water rushed into the lower room with the barrels, and it quickly came up the stairs. Raoul and the Persian tried wildly to find some way out. The water rose quickly, coming up to their knees.

They cried out for help, but there was no answer.

"Erik! Erik!" cried the Persian. "I saved your life once! In Persia, you were sentenced to death and I set you free! How can you repay me like this?"

There was no answer. Erik had taken Christine away and now the two men were alone to face their deaths.

The water was now up to their necks. They swam around, hitting and kicking at the mirrored walls. As the water neared the ceiling, they took their last breaths ...

The End of the Ghost's Love

When the Persian woke up, he found himself in a bed. Christine and Erik were looking over him. Christine gently put her hand on his head. Then Erik helped him drink a glass of water.

"What happened?" asked the Persian after he had drunk.

"My wife saved your lives," said Erik. The Persian looked at Christine, but she said nothing. He looked around the room and saw Raoul sleeping on a sofa.

"Go back to sleep," said Erik. "When you are well enough, I will take you back to your homes. I do this to please my wife. She begged for your lives and I hate to see her in pain."

The Persian was still very weak and could not stay awake. He fell back asleep trying to understand what Erik was saying.

The next time the Persian awoke, he was in his own bed at home. Darius, his servant, was there, looking after him. When he asked what had happened to him, Darius said he had found him lying in the doorway of his house last night. He had been left there by a tall stranger who wore a mask.

It took a few days for the Persian to recover. As soon as he was well enough to walk, he went to the Count of Chagny's house to see if Raoul and Philippe were all right. But when he arrived, he found out that Raoul had disappeared, and Philippe was dead. The older Chagny brother had been found by the lake under the opera.

"The visitor at the lake!" thought the Persian. "Philippe must have been trying to find Raoul. He loved his younger brother so very dearly! But how had he known to come to the lake? Perhaps he had talked to the managers of the opera, who had heard Raoul's story about Erik and hadn't believed him … Perhaps Philippe had believed him … "

The Persian went back home with sadness in his heart. He could easily imagine what had happened to Philippe. He found his way to the lake, but once there, he must have set off the alarm. Erik went and found him … Then killed him with his rope … But the Persian couldn't imagine what could have happened to Raoul, or where he could be.

The Persian reported all of this to the police, but he was laughed away. Everyone thought he was mad. Left without any other choice, he began to write down everything he knew. For days he wrote, and when he was almost finished, a visitor came to his house. Darius helped a very thin, tall man in a black cape and mask into the Persian's room. It was Erik!

He seemed very weak, and Darius had to help him walk. He sank into a chair and said quietly,

"Hello, old friend."

"Murderer!" cried the Persian. "You killed Philippe de Chagny! Now, what have you done to Raoul and Christine?"

Erik put his hand over his heart and said, "They are together now, and they are free."

"What?"

"I came to tell you that I am dying. I am dying of love for Christine! But I shall die in peace, for she has given me peace."

"What are you saying?"

"If you knew how beautiful she was when she let me kiss her ... It was the first time I ever kissed a woman. But Christine, when I kissed her ... she didn't run. She was my beautiful wife and she didn't run!"

"Where is she?" demanded the Persian. "Where is Raoul? Are they dead? Have you killed them?"

"No, not dead ... but free. How she begged for that young man's life! When the water was rising, she looked at me with her beautiful blue eyes. She said she would be my true, *living wife* if I saved you both. She said she would not kill herself. She would spend the rest of her life with me! And she meant it!"

Erik paused for a moment.

"I turned the scorpion and the water went back down. I carried you both out of there. We took care of you both until you were healthy again. That young man progressed quickly, but you, my friend, you are older and weaker. I did not know if you would make it. But you did, and when she saw that you would both live, she looked at me with such thanks in her eyes! Then ... "

Erik had to stop again, for his emotions were making him weak.

"Then ... I came near her as she looked at me with those blue eyes. She let me get closer and closer ... and ... *she let me kiss her!* Without closing her eyes or turning away, she let me kiss her on the forehead! My own mother wouldn't let me near her—she would run away and throw me my mask! Oh, how good it is to kiss someone you love! What happiness! I was so moved by it that I fell to my knees and began to cry. And do you know what she did? *She took my hand and cried with me!* Her tears fell on my face. They mixed with my own tears. We cried together! I knew it was the greatest happiness I would ever feel in my life … "

Erik was crying now and it was several minutes before he could continue. When he spoke again, it was very quietly.

"I looked at the gold ring on her finger—the ring I had given her. I took it off of her finger and put it into her hand. 'Take it!' I said. 'This is my wedding gift to you … to you and to *him*.' She looked at me with those blue eyes and asked what I meant. 'I know you love him. You can have a real life with him. I want to let you go, for you took pity on me and you cried for me!'"

Erik turned away at the memory of that moment.

"I went to Raoul where he was tied up. I

untied him. She ran to him and they kissed. But Christine turned to me ... she said thank you, and then *she kissed me!* I asked her to come back when I was dead. I wanted her to bury me with the gold ring under the opera. I asked her to wear the ring until that moment. She agreed. And that was the last time I saw her. But I am dying now, and if she keeps her promise, she will come back to me soon!"

The Persian asked no questions. He believed Erik, who sat in his room crying, remembering the most important moment of his life.

Soon, Erik rose to go. He gave the Persian a package that held all of Christine Daae's letters and a few of her belongings. He told the Persian that he believed the young couple had gone back to Christine's home town in Sweden. He also asked the Persian to let the couple know of his death by writing a simple message in the *Epoque*, the newspaper. Then, Erik left.

That was the last time the Persian saw Erik— the unhappy man who had been the Angel of

Music and the opera ghost. Three weeks later, the *Epoque* ran this single line in the personal section:

"Erik is dead."

THE END

Word List

- 本文で使われている全ての語を掲載しています（LEVEL 1、2）。ただし、LEVEL 3以上は、中学校レベルの語を含みません。
- 語形が規則変化する語の見出しは原形で示しています。不規則変化語は本文中で使われている形になっています。
- 一般的な意味を紹介していますので、一部の語で本文で実際に使われている品詞や意味と合っていないことがあります。
- 品詞は以下のように示しています。

名 名詞	代 代名詞	形 形容詞	副 副詞	動 動詞	助 助動詞
前 前置詞	接 接続詞	間 間投詞	冠 冠詞	略 略語	俗 俗語
頭 接頭語	尾 接尾語	記 記号	関 関係代名詞		

A

- **ability** 名 ①できること, (〜する)能力 ②才能
- **about to** 《be –》まさに〜しようとしている, 〜するところだ
- **academy** 名 ①アカデミー, 学士院 ②学園, 学院
- **accident** 名 ①(不慮の)事故, 災難 ②偶然
- **act** 名 行為, 行い 動 ①行動する ②機能する ③演じる
- **actor** 名 俳優, 役者
- **actually** 副 実際に, 本当に, 実は
- **add** 動 ①加える, 足す ②足し算をする ③言い添える
- **advance** 名 進歩, 前進
- **afterward** 副 その後, のちに
- **again and again** 何度も繰り返して
- **against the wall** 壁を背にして
- **aha** 間 はあ, なるほど
- **alarm** 名 ①警報, 目覚まし時計 ②驚き, 突然の恐怖
- **all** all one's life ずっと, 生まれてから all over 〜中で, 全体に亘って all right 大丈夫で, よろしい, 申し分ない all the time ずっと, いつも, その間ずっと not at all 少しも〜でない not 〜 at all 少しも[全然]〜ない once and for all これを最後にきっぱりと
- **allow** 動 ①許す, 《– … to 〜》…が〜するのを可能にする, …に〜させておく ②与える
- **alone** 熟 leave 〜 alone 〜をそっとしておく
- **although** 接 〜だけれども, 〜にもかかわらず, たとえ〜でも
- **amount** 名 ①量, 額 ②《the –》合計
- **angel** 名 ①天使 ②天使のような人
- **anger** 名 怒り
- **angrily** 副 怒って, 腹立たしげに
- **angry** 熟 get angry 腹を立てる
- **anniversary** 名 記念日, 記念祭
- **any more** 熟 not 〜 any more もう[これ以上]〜ない
- **anybody** 代 ①《疑問文・条件節で》誰か ②《否定文で》誰も (〜ない) ③《肯定文で》誰でも
- **anymore** 副 《通例否定文, 疑問文で》今はもう, これ以上, これから
- **anyone** 代 ①《疑問文・条件節で》

誰か ②《否定文で》誰も（〜ない）③《肯定文で》誰でも
- **anything else** ほかの何か
- **appear** 動①現れる, 見えてくる ②（〜のように）見える, 〜らしい appear to するように見える
- **arrange** 動①並べる, 整える ②取り決める ③準備する, 手はずを整える
- **artist** 名芸術家
- **as** 熟 as if あたかも〜のように, まるで〜みたいに as long as 〜する以上は, 〜である限りは as though あたかも〜のように, まるで〜みたいに as well as 〜と同様に just as (ちょうど)であろうとおり Please be so good as to お手数ですが〜してください so 〜 as to …するほど〜で
- **aside** 副わきへ(に), 離れて
- **asleep** 形眠って(いる状態の) fall back asleep また眠りに落ちる
- **assume** 動①仮定する, 当然のことと思う ②引き受ける
- **attention** 名注意, 集中
- **audience** 名聴衆, 視聴者
- **awake** 動①目覚めさせる ②目める 形目が覚めて
- **awoke** 動 awake（目覚めさせる）の過去

B

- **bad luck** 災難, 不運, 悪運
- **ball** 名 masked ball 仮面舞踏会
- **ballet** 名バレエ, バレエ団
- **barrel** 名たる, 1たるの分量
- **bear** 動耐える
- **beautifully** 副美しく, 立派に, 見事に
- **beauty** 名①美, 美しい人[物] ②《the-》美点

- **bedroom** 名寝室
- **beg** 動懇願する, お願いする
- **behind** 前①〜の後ろに, 〜の背後に ②〜に遅れて, 〜に劣って
- **being** 動 be（〜である）の現在分詞
- **belief** 名信じること, 信念, 信用
- **belong** 動《-to〜》〜に属する, 〜のものである
- **belonging** 名《-s》持ち物, 所有物, 財産
- **below** 前①〜より下に ②〜以下の, 〜より劣る 副下に[へ]
- **besides** 副その上, さらに
- **bit** 名《a-》少し, ちょっと
- **blame** 動とがめる, 非難する be blamed on 〜のせいにされる
- **blew** 動 blow（吹く）の過去
- **blink** 動まばたきする
- **blood** 名①血, 血液 ②血統, 家柄 ③気質 flesh and blood 肉体, 生身の人間
- **blow up** 破裂する[させる]
- **bottom** 名底, 下部, すそ野, ふもと, 最下位, 根底
- **box** 名（劇場の）ボックス席
- **box-keeper** 名ボックス席の案内係
- **branch** 名枝
- **breath** 名息, 呼吸
- **bring down** 打ち降ろす
- **builder** 名建設者
- **building** 名建物, 建造物, ビルディング
- **Buquet, Joseph** （ジョゼフ・）ビュケ《道具方主任》
- **bury** 動①埋葬する, 埋める ②覆い隠す
- **business** 熟 go about one's business 自分の仕事に取り掛かる
- **but** 熟 not 〜 but … 〜ではなくて… nothing but ただ〜だけ, 〜にす

ぎない, 〜のほかは何も…ない

C

- □ **call back** 呼び返す
- □ **call for** 〜を呼び出す
- □ **call in** 〜に立ち寄る
- □ **call out** 叫ぶ, 呼び出す, 声を掛ける
- □ **calm** 形 穏やかな, 落ち着いた 動 静まる, 静める　calm down 静まる
- □ **cancel** 動 取り消す, 中止する
- □ **cape** 名 岬
- □ **care** 熟 care for 〜の世話をする, 〜を扱う, 〜が好きである, 〜を大事に思う　take care of 〜の世話をする, 〜面倒を見る, 〜を管理する
- □ **career** 名 ①(生涯の・専門的な)職業 ②経歴, キャリア　high point of someone's career キャリアの頂点
- □ **Carlotta** 名 カルロッタ《スター歌手》
- □ **carriage** 名 ①馬車 ②乗り物, 車
- □ **Cecile Jammes** セシル・ジャム《若いバレリーナ》
- □ **ceiling** 名 天井
- □ **cellar** 名 地下貯蔵室
- □ **certain** 形 ある
- □ **chandelier** 名 シャンデリア
- □ **chapter** 名 (書物の)章
- □ **charge** 名 責任　in charge of 〜を任されて, 〜を担当して, 〜の責任を負って
- □ **check** 動 検査する
- □ **chief** 名 頭, 長, 親分
- □ **child-like** 形 子どものような
- □ **child's play** 非常に簡単なこと, 朝飯前のこと
- □ **chocolate** 名 チョコレート
- □ **choice** 名 選択(の範囲・自由)
- □ **Christine Daae** クリスティーヌ・ダーエ《オペラ座の歌手》
- □ **clear** 形 ①はっきりした, 明白な ②澄んだ ③(よく)晴れた 動 ①はっきりさせる ②片づける ③晴れる
- □ **clearly** 副 ①明らかに, はっきりと ②《返答に用いて》そのとおり
- □ **climb into** 〜に乗り込む
- □ **close 〜 behind** …を〜の後ろで閉める
- □ **closely** 副 ①密接に ②念入りに, 詳しく ③ぴったりと
- □ **closer and closer** どんどん近づく
- □ **clothing** 名 衣類, 衣料品
- □ **co-ack** 間 クワック《ヒキガエルのような鳴き声》
- □ **coffin** 名 棺
- □ **come down** 下りて来る
- □ **come into** 〜に入ってくる
- □ **come out** 出てくる, 出掛ける, 姿を現す
- □ **come up** 近づいてくる, 階上に行く
- □ **concerned** 形 心配そうな, 気にしている
- □ **connect** 動 つながる, つなぐ, 関係づける
- □ **connection** 名 ①つながり, 関係 ②縁故
- □ **contract** 名 契約(書), 協定
- □ **control** 動 ①管理[支配]する ②抑制する, コントロールする
- □ **correct** 形 正しい, 適切な, りっぱな
- □ **could** 熟 How could 〜? 何だって〜なんてことがありえようか？　could have done 〜だったかもしれない《仮定法》
- □ **count** 動 ①数える ②(〜を…と)みなす ③重要[大切]である 名 伯爵
- □ **couple** 名 ①2つ, 対 ②夫婦, 一組

Word List

③数個 a couple of 2, 3の
- **cover** 動覆う, 包む, 隠す
- **crash** 動大きな音を立ててぶつかる［壊れる］
- **crawl** 動はう, 腹ばいで進む, ゆっくり進む
- **create** 動創造する, 生み出す, 引き起こす
- **crowd** 動群がる, 混雑する crowd around ～の周りに集まる 名群集, 雑踏, 多数, 聴衆
- **crowded** 形混雑した, 満員の
- **cry out** 叫ぶ
- **cursed** 動のろわれた
- **cut down** 切り倒す, 打ちのめす

D

- **Daae, Christine** 《クリスティーヌ・》ダーエ《オペラ座の歌手》
- **dancer** 名踊り子, ダンサー
- **dare** 動《- to ～》思い切って［あえて］～する
- **Darius** 名ダリウス《「ペルシャ人」の召使い》
- **darkness** 名暗さ, 暗やみ
- **de** 《フランス語》= from, of
- **de Chagny** ド・シャニー《人名》
- **deal** 動《- with [in]》～を扱う
- **dearly** 副とても, 心から
- **death** 名①死, 死ぬこと ②《the -》終えん, 消滅 be sentenced to death 死刑判決を受ける
- **Debienne, Mr.** ドビエンヌ氏《オペラ座の前支配人》
- **deep-set** 形深くくぼんだ, (目が)奥まった
- **demand** 動①要求する, 尋ねる ②必要とする 名①要求, 請求 ②需要

- **demanding** 形要求が厳しい
- **depend** 動《- on [upon] ～》①～を頼る, ～をあてにする ②～による
- **describe** (言葉で)描写する, 特色を述べる, 説明する
- **description** 名(言葉で)記述(すること), 描写(すること)
- **detail** 名細部, 《-s》詳細
- **device** 名①工夫 ②案 ③装置
- **die of** ～がもとで死ぬ
- **difficulty** 名①むずかしさ ②難局, 支障, 苦情, 異議 ③《-ties》財政困難
- **disappear** 動見えなくなる, 姿を消す, なくなる
- **disappearance** 名見えなくなること, 消失, 失踪
- **discuss** 動議論[検討]する
- **doing** 名①すること, したこと ②《-s》行為, 出来事
- **Don Juan Triumphant** 「勝ち誇るドン・ジョバンニ」《曲名》
- **doorway** 名戸口, 玄関, 出入り口
- **double** 動①2倍になる[する] ②兼ねる
- **doubt** 動疑う
- **drag** 動①引きずる ②のろのろ動く[動かす]
- **draw up** (車を)止める
- **drawn** 動 draw (引く)の過去分詞
- **dressing room** 楽屋
- **drug** 名薬, 麻薬, 麻酔薬
- **dying** 形死にかかっている, 消えそうな

E

- **each other** お互いに
- **earn** 動①儲ける, 稼ぐ ②(名声を)博す
- **easily** 副①容易に, たやすく, 苦も

- [ ] **edge** 名 ①刃 ②端, 縁
- [ ] **either A or B** AかそれともB
- [ ] **emotion** 名 感激, 感動, 感情
- [ ] **end up** 結局〜になる
- [ ] **engage** 動 ①約束する, 婚約する ②雇う, 従事する[させる], 《be -d in》〜に従事している
- [ ] **entire** 形 全体の, 完全な, まったくの
- [ ] **entirely** 副 完全に, まったく
- [ ] **Epoque** 名 「エポック」紙
- [ ] **Erik** 名 エリック《人名》
- [ ] **escape** 動 逃げる, 免れる
- [ ] **ever since** それ以来ずっと
- [ ] **everybody** 代 誰でも, 皆
- [ ] **everyone** 代 誰でも, 皆
- [ ] **everything** 代 すべてのこと[もの], 何でも, 何もかも
- [ ] **everywhere** 副 どこにいても, いたるところに
- [ ] **evidence** 名 ①証拠, 証人 ②形跡
- [ ] **examiner** 名 試験管, 審査員
- [ ] **excellence** 名 優秀さ, 卓越, 長所
- [ ] **excellent** 形 優れた, 優秀な
- [ ] **except** 前 〜を除いて, 〜のほかは except for 〜を除いて, 〜がなければ
- [ ] **excited** 形 興奮した, わくわくした
- [ ] **exist** 動 存在する, 生存する, ある, いる
- [ ] **expect** 動 予期[予測]する, (当然のこととして)期待する
- [ ] **explosion** 名 爆発, 急増
- [ ] **express** 動 表現する, 述べる
- [ ] **extra** 形 余分の, 臨時の

F

- [ ] **fact** 熟 in fact つまり, 実は, 要するに
- [ ] **fail** 動 失敗する
- [ ] **faint** 動 気絶する
- [ ] **fall back asleep** また眠りに落ちる
- [ ] **fall on** 〜に降りかかる
- [ ] **fallen** 動 fall (落ちる) の過去分詞
- [ ] **fame** 名 評判, 名声
- [ ] **Faust** 名 『ファウスト』《シャルル・グノーが作曲した全5幕のオペラ》
- [ ] **fear** 名 ①恐れ ②心配, 不安
- [ ] **feature** 名 ①特徴, 特色 ②顔の一部, 《-s》顔立ち
- [ ] **figure out** 理解する, 〜であるとわかる, (原因などを)解明する
- [ ] **final** 形 最後の, 決定的な
- [ ] **find one's way** たどり着く
- [ ] **find out** 見つけ出す, 気がつく, 知る, 調べる, 解明する
- [ ] **firmly** 副 しっかりと, 断固として
- [ ] **first sight** 《at -》一目見て
- [ ] **fit** 名 発作, けいれん, 一時的興奮 in a fit of madness 錯乱状態になって
- [ ] **flesh** 名 肉, 《the -》肉体 flesh and blood 肉体, 生身の人間
- [ ] **flow** 動 流れ出る, 流れる, あふれる
- [ ] **following** 形 《the -》次の, 次に続く
- [ ] **foolish** 形 おろかな, ばかばかしい
- [ ] **footstep** 名 足音, 歩み
- [ ] **forehead** 名 ひたい
- [ ] **forgive** 動 許す, 免除する
- [ ] **foyer** 名 控え室 foyer de ballet バレリーナ共同控え室
- [ ] **franc** 名 フラン《フランスで使用されていた通貨単位》
- [ ] **France** 名 フランス《国名》

WORD LIST

- **free** 熟 set free (人)を解放する, 釈放される, 自由の身になる
- **French** 名 ①フランス語 ②《the -》フランス人
- **frightening** 形 恐ろしい, どきっとさせる
- **front of**《in -》～の前に, ～の正面に

G

- **Gabriel** 名 ガブリエル《声楽主任》
- **gather** 動 ①集まる, 集める ②生じる, 増す ③推測する
- **genius** 名 天才, 才能
- **gently** 副 親切に, 上品に, そっと, 優しく
- **get** 熟 get angry 腹を立てる get into ～に入る, 入り込む get on one's knee 片膝をつく get out of ～から外へ出る[抜け出る] get there そこに到着する get tired 疲れる get tired of ～に飽きる, ～が嫌になる get to (事)を始める, ～に達する[到着する] get to do できるようになる, ～できる機会を得る
- **ghost** 名 幽霊
- **gift** 名 贈り物
- **Giry, little** (メグ・)ジリー《若いバレリーナ》
- **Giry, Mrs.** ジリー夫人《ボックス席の案内係》
- **give out** 動 かなくなる
- **go** 熟 go about one's business 自分の仕事に取り掛かる go away 立ち去る go down 下に降りる go missing 行方不明になる go out 外出する, 外へ出る go over ～を見直す, 練習する go sailing 帆走する go walking 散歩に出掛ける go wild 狂乱する
- **gold** 名 金, 金貨, 金製品, 金色 形 金の, 金製の, 金色の
- **golden** 形 ①金色の ②金製の ③貴重な
- **good** 熟 Please be so good as to お手数ですが～してください leave someone for good 永遠に(人)と別れる
- **grab** 動 ①ふいにつかむ, ひったくる ②横取りする
- **grand staircase** 大階段
- **grasshopper** 名 バッタ(飛蝗)《昆虫》
- **greatly** 副 大いに
- **greet** 動 ①あいさつする ②(喜んで)迎える
- **guest** 名 客, ゲスト
- **gun** 名 銃

H

- **hall** 名 公会堂, ホール, 大広間, 玄関
- **hand** 熟 have one's hand in marriage 結婚を申し込む on the other hand 一方, 他方では
- **hang** 動 かかる, かける, つるす, ぶら下がる hang on ～につかまる, しがみつく
- **happen to** たまたま～する, 偶然～する
- **happily** 副 幸福に, 楽しく, うまく, 幸いにも
- **happiness** 名 幸せ, 喜び
- **hardly** 副 ①ほとんど～でない, わずかに ②厳しく, かろうじて
- **hat peg** 名 帽子掛け
- **hate** 動 嫌う, 憎む, (～するのを)いやがる
- **hatred** 名 憎しみ, 毛嫌い
- **haunting** 形 記憶に長く残る
- **have** 熟 could have done ～だったかもしれない《仮定法》have one's hand in marriage 結婚を申

THE PHANTOM OF THE OPERA

し込む **have power over** ～を思いのままに操る力を持っている **have something to say** 言いたいことがある **should have done** ～すべきだった（のにしなかった）《仮定法》 **will have done** ～してしまっているだろう《未来完了形》

- **healthy** 形 健康な, 健全な, 健康によい
- **hear of** ～について聞く
- **heat** 名 熱, 暑さ
- **heaven** 名 天国
- **height** 名 高さ, 身長
- **helpful** 形 役に立つ, 参考になる
- **hid** 動 hide（隠れる）の過去, 過去分詞
- **hidden** 形 隠れた, 秘密の
- **hide** 動 隠れる, 隠す, 隠れて見えない, 秘密にする
- **high point of someone's career** キャリアの頂点
- **hire** 動 雇う
- **hold** 熟 hold ～ out in front of ～を…の前に差し出す take hold of ～をつかむ, 捕らえる, 制する
- **honestly** 副 正直に
- **hopeless** 形 ①希望のない, 絶望的な ②勝ち目のない
- **horrible** 形 恐ろしい, ひどい
- **How could ～?** 何だって～なんてことがありえようか？
- **however** 副 たとえ～でも 接 けれども, だが
- **huge** 形 巨大な, ばく大な
- **hung** 動 hang（かかる）の過去, 過去分詞
- **hurry down** 急いで下りる［駆け込む］

I

- **imagine** 動 想像する, 心に思い描く
- **impress** 動 印象づける, 感銘させる
- **inch** 名 ①インチ《長さの単位。1/12フィート, 2.54cm》②少量
- **including** 前 ～を含めて, 込みで
- **indeed** 副 実際, 本当に
- **India** 名 インド《国名》
- **ink** 名 インク
- **inn** 名 宿屋, 居酒屋
- **institution** 名 協会, 公共団体
- **intermission** 名 ①休止, 中断 ②幕間,（劇場・映画館などの）休憩時間
- **iron** 名 鉄, 鉄製のもの
- **Isidore Saak** イジドール・サーク《マニエラ夫妻の友人》

J

- **Jammes, little** （セシル・）ジャンム《若いバレリーナ》
- **jealous** 形 嫉妬して, 嫉妬深い, うらやんで
- **jewelry** 名 宝石, 宝飾品類
- **joke** 名 冗談, ジョーク 動 冗談を言う, ふざける, からかう
- **Joseph Buquet** ジョゼフ・ビュケ《道具方主任》
- **joy** 名 喜び, 楽しみ
- **Julie** 名 ジュリー《マニエラ夫人の名》
- **just as** （ちょうど）であろうとおり
- **just then** そのとたんに

K

- **keep one's promise** 約束を守

WORD LIST

る
- **kidnapping** 名誘拐
- **kiss** 名キス 動キスする
- **knee** 名ひざ get on one's knee 片膝をつく
- **knock** 動ノックする, たたく, ぶつける
- **know** 熟 let someone know of (人)に知らせる

L

- **la** 冠フランス語の女性名詞につく定冠詞
- **lamp** 名ランプ, 灯火
- **last** 熟 at the last minute 直前に the last time この前~したとき
- **latest** 形最新の, 最近の
- **laughter** 名笑い(声)
- **lay** 動 lie (横たわる)の過去
- **lead the way** 先に立って導く, 案内する, 率先する
- **lead to** ~に至る, ~に通じる, ~を引き起こす
- **leave** 熟 leave someone for good 永遠に(人)と別れる leave ~ alone ~をそっとしておく make someone leave 退職させる
- **led** 動 lead (導く)の過去, 過去分詞
- **let someone know of** 熟(人)に知らせる
- **level** 名階
- **lie** 動①うそをつく ②横たわる, 寝る ③(ある状態に)ある, 存在する
- **life** 熟 all one's life ずっと, 生まれてから
- **lift** 動持ち上げる
- **list** 動名簿[目録]に記入する
- **living** 形①生きている, 現存の ②使用されている
- **living room** 居間
- **lock** 名巻き毛, 髪の房
- **lonely** 形①孤独な, 心さびしい ②ひっそりした, 人里離れた
- **long** 熟 as long as ~する以上は, ~である限りは
- **look after** ~の世話をする
- **look for** ~を探す
- **look over** ~越しに見る, ~を見渡す
- **look through** ~をのぞき込む
- **look up** 見上げる, 調べる
- **lovely** 形愛らしい, 美しい, すばらしい
- **lover** 名①愛人, 恋人 ②愛好者
- **luck** 熟 bad luck 災難, 不運, 悪運
- **lying** 動 lie (うそをつく・横たわる)の現在分詞

M

- **mad** 形①気の狂った ②逆上した, 理性をなくした ③ばかげた ④(~に)熱狂[熱中]して, 夢中の
- **made to** 熟《be-》~させられる
- **madness** 名狂気, 熱中 in a fit of madness 錯乱状態になって
- **maid** 名お手伝い, メイド
- **main** 形主な, 主要な
- **make** 熟 make it 回復する make noise 音を立てる make one's way 進む, 行く make sense 意味をなす, よくわかる make someone leave 退職させる what to make of ~をどう判断するか
- **manager** 名経営者, 支配人, 支店長, 部長
- **Maniera, Mr. and Mrs.** マニエラ夫妻《宝石商》
- **many** 熟 so many 非常に多くの
- **Margarita** 名マルグリート《『フ

THE PHANTOM OF THE OPERA

ァゥスト』のヒロイン》

- **marriage** 名 ①結婚(生活・式) ②結合, 融合, (吸収)合併 have one's hand in marriage 結婚を申し込む
- **marry** 動 結婚する
- **mask** 名 面, マスク
- **masked ball** 仮面舞踏会
- **master** 名 主人, 雇い主, 師, 名匠
- **masterpiece** 名 傑作, 名作, 代表作
- **matter** 熟 a matter of ~の問題 no matter ~を問わず, どうでもいい
- **May I ~?** ~してもよいですか。
- **mean** 動 本気である
- **meanwhile** 副 それまでの間, 一方では
- **Meg Giry** メグ・ジリー《若いバレリーナ》
- **memory** 名 記憶(力), 思い出
- **midnight** 名 夜の12時, 真夜中, 暗黒
- **might** 動《mayの過去》①~かもしれない ②~してもよい, ~できる
- **mind** 名 ①心, 精神, 考え ②知性 動 ①気にする, いやがる ②気をつける, 用心する Never mind. 気にするな。
- **minister** 名 ①大臣, 閣僚, 公使 ②聖職者
- **minute** 熟 at the last minute 直前に
- **mirror** 名 鏡
- **mirrored** 形 鏡張りの
- **missing** 形 欠けている, 行方不明の go missing 行方不明になる
- **mix** 動 ①混ざる, 混ぜる ②(~を)一緒にする
- **moment** 名 ①瞬間, ちょっとの間 ②(特定の)時, 時期 for a moment 少しの間 in a moment ただちに
- **Moncharmin, Mr.** モンシャル

マン氏《オペラ座の新支配人》
- **monster** 名 怪物
- **more** 熟 not ~ any more もう[これ以上]~ない
- **morning** 熟 one morning ある朝
- **moved** 形 感激する, 感銘する
- **moving** 形 動いている
- **murderer** 名 殺人犯
- **musical** 形 音楽の
- **musician** 名 音楽家
- **mystery** 名 神秘, 不可思議

N

- **nail** 名 くぎ, びょう
- **narrow** 形 狭い
- **national** 形 国家[国民]の, 全国の
- **National Academy of Music** 国立高等音楽院
- **nearby** 副 近くで, 間近で
- **neither** 代 (2者のうち)どちらも~でない
- **Never mind.** 気にするな。
- **newspaper** 名 新聞(紙)
- **next time** 次回に
- **next to** ~のとなりに, ~の次に
- **no** 熟 no matter ~を問わず, どうでもいい no one 誰も[一人も]~ない with no regard to ~を気にせずに
- **nobody** 代 誰も[1人も]~ない
- **noise** 名 騒音, 騒ぎ, 物音 make noise 音を立てる
- **not at all** 少しも~でない
- **not quite** まったく~だというわけではない
- **not ~ any more** もう[これ以上]~ない
- **not ~ at all** 少しも[全然]~ない

WORD LIST

- **not ~ but ...** ~ではなくて…
- **note** 名 ①メモ, 覚え書き ②音符
- **nothing but** ただ～だけ, ～にすぎない, ～のほかは何も…ない
- **notice** 名 ①注意 ②通知 ③公告 動 ①気づく, 認める ②通告する
- **notify** 動 知らせる, 通知する, 報告する, 届け出る
- **now** 熟 for now 今のところ, ひとまず

O

- **object** 名 物, 事物
- **occasion** 名 ①場合, (特定の)時 ②機会, 好機 ③理由, 根拠
- **odd** 形 ①奇妙な ②奇数の ③(一対のうちの)片方の
- **off** 形 基準から離れた[はずれた]
- **offer** 名 提案, 提供
- **old wives' tale** 愚かな迷信
- **once** 熟 at once すぐに, 同時に once and for all これを最後にきっぱりと
- **one** 熟 no one 誰も[一人も]～ない one by one 1つずつ, 1人ずつ one day (過去の)ある日, (未来の)いつか one morning ある朝
- **oneself** 熟 《by –》一人で, 自分だけで
- **onto** 前 ～の上へ[に]
- **open up** 広がる, 広げる, 開く, 開ける
- **opera** 名 歌劇, オペラ
- **organ** 名 (パイプ)オルガン
- **other** 熟 each other お互いに on the other hand 一方, 他方では
- **over** 熟 all over ～中で, 全体に亘って be over 終わる go over ～を見直す, 練習する have power over ～を思いのままに操る力を持っている look over ～越しに見る, ～を見渡す take over 引き継ぐ, 支配する, 乗っ取る win over 説得する, 口説き落とす
- **owner** 名 持ち主, オーナー

P

- **package** 名 包み, 小包, パッケージ
- **paid** 動 pay (払う)の過去, 過去分詞
- **pair** 名 (2つから成る)一対, 一組, ペア
- **pale** 形 (顔色・人が)青ざめた, 青白い
- **Paris Opera House** パリ・オペラ座
- **Parisian** 形 パリ人の
- **partly** 副 一部分は, ある程度は
- **party** 熟 throw a party パーティーを開く
- **pass away** 死ぬ
- **past** 前 《時間・場所》～を過ぎて, ～を越して 副 通り越して, 過ぎて walk past 通り過ぎる
- **pause** 動 休止する, 立ち止まる
- **pay** 動 支払う, 払う, 報いる
- **peace** 名 《in –》安らかに
- **peg** 名 (帽子などをかける)くぎ, 木くぎ, くさび, 留めくぎ
- **perfectly** 副 完全に, 申し分なく
- **perform** 動 ①(任務などを)行う, 果たす, 実行する ②演じる, 演奏する
- **performance** 名 ①実行, 行為 ②成績, できばえ, 業績 ③演劇, 演奏, 見世物
- **perhaps** 副 たぶん, ことによると
- **Perros** ペロス《フランスの地名》
- **Persia** 名 ペルシア《国名。現在のイ

ラン》
- **Persian** 形 ペルシア(語)の 名 ①ペルシア人 ②ペルシア語
- **persian hat** アストラカン帽《子羊(特にロシアのアストラカン地方産)の毛皮でできた黒い帽子》のこと
- **personal** 形 ①個人の, 私的な ②本人自らの
- **phantom** 名 幽霊, 幻影
- **Philippe de Chagny, Count** フィリップ・ド・シャニー伯爵《ラウルの兄》
- **physically** 副 ①自然法則上, 物理的に ②肉体的に, 身体的に
- **pity** 名 哀れみ, 同情, 残念なこと **take pity on** ~に同情を示す, ~を哀れむ 動 気の毒に思う, 哀れむ
- **place** take one's place (人と)交代する, (人)の代わりをする, 後任になる take place 行われる, 起こる
- **plainly** 副 はっきりと, 明らかに
- **play** 熟 child's play 非常に簡単なこと, 朝飯前のこと
- **player** 名 ①競技者, 選手, 演奏者, 俳優 ②演奏装置
- **pleasant** 形 ①(物事が)楽しい, 心地よい ②快活な, 愛想のよい
- **point** 熟 high point of someone's career キャリアの頂点
- **Poligny, Mr.** ポリニー氏《オペラ座の前支配人》
- **politely** 副 ていねいに, 上品に
- **position** 名 ①位置, 場所, 姿勢 ②地位, 身分, 職 ③立場, 状況
- **possible** 形 ①可能な ②ありうる, 起こりうる
- **possibly** 副 ①あるいは, たぶん ②《否定文, 疑問文で》どうしても, できる限り, とても, なんとか
- **powder** 名 粉末, 火薬
- **power** 熟 have power over ~を思いのままに操る力を持っている
- **praise** 動 ほめる, 賞賛する
- **president** 名 ①大統領 ②社長, 学長, 頭取
- **press** 圧する, 押す
- **private** 形 私的な, 個人の
- **probably** 副 たぶん, あるいは
- **professor** 名 教授, 師匠
- **progress** 動 前進する, 上達する
- **prologue** 名 プロローグ, 序言, 前触れ
- **promise** 熟 keep one's promise 約束を守る
- **proud** 形 ①自慢の, 誇った, 自尊心のある ②高慢な, 尊大な **be proud of** ~を自慢に思う
- **proudly** 副 ①誇らしげに ②うぬぼれて
- **prove** 動 ①証明する ②(~であることが)わかる, (~と)なる
- **pull away** 引き離す, もぎ取る
- **pull out** 引き出す, 取り出す
- **pure** 形 ①純粋な, 混じりけのない ②罪のない, 清い
- **put on** ①~を身につける, 着る ②~を…の上に置く
- **put one's name on the line** 欄に署名する
- **put out** ①外に出す, (手など)を(差し)出す

Q

- **quality** 名 ①質, 性質, 品質 ②特性 ③良質
- **quickly** 副 敏速に, 急いで
- **quietly** 副 ①静かに ②平穏に, 控えめに
- **quite** 熟 not quite まったく~だというわけではない

WORD LIST

R

- **Raoul de Chagny, Viscount** ラウル・ド・シャニー子爵
- **rather** 副 ①むしろ、かえって ②かなり、いくぶん、やや ③それどころか逆に
- **reach out** 手を伸ばす
- **reach up** 背伸びをする
- **ready to**《be –》すぐに［いつでも］～できる、～する構えで
- **realize** 動 理解する、実現する
- **recognize** 動 認める、認識［承認］する
- **recover** 動 ①取り戻す、ばん回する ②回復する
- **red** 熟 turn red 赤くなる
- **Red Death** 赤い死神、赤死病（天然痘）
- **refuse** 動 拒絶する、断る
- **regard** 名 注意、関心 with no regard to ～を気にせずに
- **release** 動 解き放す
- **relief** 名 （苦痛・心配などの）除去、軽減、安心、気晴らし
- **remain** 動 ①残っている、残る ②（～の）ままである［いる］
- **remove** 動 ①取り去る、除去する ②（衣類を）脱ぐ
- **repay** 動 ①払い戻す、返金する ②報いる、恩返しする
- **reply** 動 答える、返事をする、応答する 名 答え、返事、応答
- **respect** 動 尊敬［尊重］する
- **responsible** 形 責任のある、信頼できる、確実な
- **retirement** 名 引退、退職
- **retiring** 形 退職した
- **Richard, Mr.** リシェール氏《オペラ座の新支配人》
- **ring** 名 指輪
- **ringing** 形 鳴り響く、鳴りわたる
- **Roi de Lahore**『ラホールの王』《ジュール・マスネが作曲したオペラ》
- **role** 名 ①（劇などの）役 ②役割、任務
- **roof** 名 屋根（のようなもの）
- **rope** 名 綱、なわ、ロープ
- **run away** 走り去る、逃げ出す
- **run up** ～に走り寄る
- **rush** 動 突進する、せき立てる 名 突進、殺到 in a rush 大急ぎで

S

- **Saack, Isidore** （イジドール・）サーク《マニエラ夫妻の友人》
- **sadly** 副 悲しそうに、不幸にも
- **sadness** 名 悲しみ、悲哀
- **safely** 副 安全に、間違いなく
- **safety** 名 安全、無事、確実
- **sail** 動 帆走する、航海する、出航する
- **sailing** 熟 go sailing 帆走する
- **sailor** 名 船員、（ヨットの）乗組員
- **sank** 動 sink (沈む) の過去
- **scarf** 名 スカーフ
- **scene-changer** 名 大道具方
- **scorpion** 名 サソリ（蠍）
- **sea-side** 形 海辺の
- **search** 動 捜し求める、調べる
- **secret** 名 秘密、神秘
- **secretly** 副 秘密に、内緒で
- **see if** ～かどうかを確かめる
- **seem** 動 （～に）見える、（～のように）思われる seem to be ～であるように思われる
- **send for** ～を呼びにやる、～を呼び寄せる
- **sense** 名 ①感覚、感じ ②《-s》意識、正気、本性 ③常識、分別、センス ④

THE PHANTOM OF THE OPERA

- 意味 make sense 意味をなす，よくわかる
- **sentence** 名 ①文 ②判決，宣告 動 判決を下す，宣告する be sentenced to death 死刑判決を受ける
- **serious** 形 ①まじめな，真剣な ②重大な，深刻な，(病気などが)重い
- **servant** 名 ①召使，使用人，しもべ ②公務員，(公共事業の)従業員
- **set free** (人)を解放する，釈放される，自由の身になる
- **set off** 作動する［させる］
- **set piece** 大道具
- **settle** 動 ①安定する［させる］，落ち着く，落ち着かせる ②《 in ~ 》~に移り住む，定住する
- **shadow** 名 ①影，暗がり ②亡霊
- **shake** 動 ①振る，揺れる，揺さぶる，震える ②動揺させる shake off 振り払う
- **Shall we ~?** (一緒に)~しましょうか．
- **shine** 動 光る，輝く
- **shocked** 形 ~にショックを受けて，憤慨して
- **shone** 動 shine (光る)の過去，過去分詞
- **shook** 動 shake (振る)の過去
- **shore** 名 岸，海岸，陸
- **should have done** ~すべきだった(のにしなかった)《仮定法》
- **shoulder** 名 肩 throw back one's shoulders 胸を張る
- **shown** 動 show (見せる)の過去分詞
- **shut** 動 ①閉まる，閉める，閉じる ②たたむ ③閉じ込める ④shutの過去，過去分詞
- **shy** 形 内気な，恥ずかしがりの，臆病な
- **Siebel** 名 ジーベル《『ファウスト』の登場人物》
- **sight** 熟 at first sight 一目見て
- **silence** 名 沈黙，無言，静寂
- **silent** 形 ①無言の，黙っている ②静かな，音を立てない ③活動しない
- **simply** 副 ①簡単に ②単に，ただ ③まったく，完全に
- **since** 熟 ever since それ以来ずっと
- **singer** 名 歌手，シンガー
- **singing** 名 歌うこと，歌声
- **single** 形 たった1つの
- **sit up** 起き上がる，上半身を起こす
- **six-sided** 形 6面の
- **skeleton** 名 骨格，がい骨
- **skilled** 形 熟練した，腕のいい，熟練を要する
- **skull** 名 頭蓋骨，頭，頭脳
- **slight** 形 ①わずかな ②ほっそりして ③とるに足らない
- **slip** 動 滑る，滑らせる slip away すり抜ける，こっそり去る，静かに立ち去る
- **slowly** 副 遅く，ゆっくり
- **so** 熟 Please be so good as to お手数ですが~してください and so そこで，それだから，それで and so on ~など，その他もろもろ so many 非常に多くの so ~ as to … …するほど~で so ~ that … 非常に~なので…
- **sofa** 名 ソファー
- **soften** 動 柔らかくなる［する］，和らぐ
- **softly** 副 柔らかに，優しく，そっと
- **soldier** 名 兵士，兵卒
- **some** 熟 for some time しばらくの間
- **somebody** 代 誰か，ある人
- **someday** 副 いつか，そのうち
- **somehow** 副 ①どうにかこうにか

WORD LIST

か, ともかく, 何とかして ②どういうわけか
- **someone** 代 ある人, 誰か
- **something** 代 ①ある物, 何か ②いくぶん, 多少
- **sometimes** 副 時々, 時たま
- **somewhere** 副 ①どこかへ[に] ②いつか, およそ
- **song-master** 名 声楽主任
- **Sorelli** 名 ソレリ《プリマ・バレリーナ》
- **soul** 名 ①魂 ②精神, 心
- **spirit** 名 ①霊 ②精神, 気力
- **splendid** 形 見事な, 壮麗な, 堂々とした
- **spot** 名 地点, 場所
- **stage** 名 ①舞台 ②段階
- **stage-box** 名 特別ボックス席
- **stair** 名 ①(階段の)1段 ②《-s》階段, はしご
- **staircase** 名 階段
- **stand by** そばに立つ, 傍観する, 待機する
- **stare** 動 じっと[じろじろ]見る
- **state** 動 述べる, 表明する
- **steal** 動 ①盗む ②こっそりと手に入れる, こっそりと~する
- **stick** 動 突き出る stick out of ~から突き出す
- **stone** 名 ①石, 小石 ②宝石
- **stop by** 途中で立ち寄る, ちょっと訪ねる
- **stranger** 名 ①見知らぬ人, 他人 ②不案内[不慣れ]な人
- **strangler** 名 絞殺魔
- **struck** 動 strike (打つ) の過去, 過去分詞
- **struggle** 動 もがく, 奮闘する
- **such ~ that ...** 非常に~なので...

- **sudden** 形 突然の, 急な
- **sunset** 名 日没, 夕焼け
- **suppose** 動 ①仮定する, 推測する ②《be -d to ~》~することになっている, ~するものである
- **surely** 副 確かに, きっと
- **surprised** 形 驚いた
- **swam** 動 swim (泳ぐ) の過去
- **sweat** 動 汗をかく
- **Sweden** 名 スウェーデン《国名》
- **Swedish** 形 スウェーデン人[語]の 名 スウェーデン語,《the -》スウェーデン人
- **sword** 名 剣, 刀

T

- **take** 熟 take away ①連れ去る ②取り上げる, 奪い去る ③取り除く take care of ~の世話をする, ~面倒を見る, ~を管理する take hold of ~をつかむ, 捕らえる, 制する take off (衣服を)脱ぐ, 取り去る, ~を取り除く, 離陸する, 出発する take one's place (人と)交代する, (人の)代わりをする, 後任になる take over 引き継ぐ, 支配する, 乗っ取る take pity on ~に同情を示す, ~を哀れむ take place 行われる, 起こる take someone away (人)を連れ出す take up (時間・場所を)とる, 占める
- **tale** 名 ①話, 物語 ②うわさ, 悪口 old wives' tale 愚かな迷信
- **talk of** ~のことを話す
- **tear off** 引きはがす
- **terribly** 副 ひどく
- **that** 熟 after that その後 so ~ that ... 非常に~なので... such ~ that ... 非常に~なので...
- **then** 熟 by then その時までに just then そのとたんに
- **there** 熟 get there そこに到着する

107

THE PHANTOM OF THE OPERA

- **thin** 形 薄い, 細い, やせた, まばらな
- **think of** ~のことを考える, ~を思いつく, 考え出す
- **third-floor** 形 3階の
- **this** 熟 at this これを見て, そこで(すぐに) by this time この時までに, もうすでに in this way このようにして this way このように
- **though** 接 ①~にもかかわらず, ~だが ②たとえ~でも as though あたかも~のように, まるで~みたいに 副 しかし
- **threat** 名 おどし, 脅迫
- **throughout** 前 ①~中, ~を通じて ②~のいたるところに
- **throw a party** パーティーを開く
- **throw back one's shoulders** 胸を張る
- **tie up** ひもで縛る, 縛り上げる, つなぐ, 拘束する
- **tight** 副 堅く, しっかりと
- **tightly** 副 きつく, しっかり, 堅く
- **time** 熟 all the time ずっと, いつも, その間ずっと at the time そのころ, 当時は by the time ~する時までに by this time この時までに, もうすでに for some time しばらくの間 next time 次回 the last time この前~したとき
- **tired** 形 ①疲れた, くたびれた ②あきた, うんざりした be tired of ~に飽きて[うんざりして]いる get tired 疲れる get tired of ~に飽きる, ~が嫌になる
- **tore** 動 tear (裂く)の過去
- **torture** 名 (肉体的な)苦痛を与えること, 拷問 動 拷問にかける, ひどく苦しめる
- **total** 形 総計の, 全体の, 完全な 名 全体, 合計
- **totally** 副 全体的に, すっかり
- **trap** 動 わなを仕掛ける, わなで捕らえる
- **trap-door** 名 秘密の抜け穴
- **trip** 動 つまづく
- **truly** 副 ①全く, 本当に, 真に ②心から, 誠実に
- **truth** 名 ①真理, 事実, 本当 ②誠実, 忠実さ
- **turn** 熟 turn around 振り向く, 向きを変える, 方向転換する turn away 向こうへ行く, 追い払う, (顔を)そむける, 横を向く turn back 元に戻る 拒絶する turn into 進路を~へ向ける turn off (照明などを)消す turn on (照明などを)つける turn red 赤くなる turn white 青ざめる, 血の気が引く

U

- **ugly** 形 ①醜い, ぶかっこうな ②いやな, 不快な, 険悪な
- **unable** 形 《be – to ~》~することができない
- **unbelievable** 形 信じられない(ほどの), 度のはずれた
- **unconscious** 形 無意識の, 気絶した
- **underground** 形 ①地下の[にある] ②地下組織の ③前衛的な 名 ①地下鉄, 地下(道) ②地下組織 ③前衛運動
- **unhappy** 形 不運な, 不幸な
- **unlike** 形 似ていない, 違った 前 ~と違って
- **untie** 動 ほどく, 解放する
- **up to** ~まで, ~に至るまで, ~に匹敵して
- **used to** よく~したものだ, 以前は~であった

WORD LIST

V

- □ **value** 動評価する, 値をつける, 大切にする
- □ **version** 名バージョン, 版, 翻訳
- □ **violin** 名バイオリン
- □ **viscount** 名子爵
- □ **vision** 名①視力 ②先見, 洞察力
- □ **visitor** 名訪問客
- □ **vivacity** 名活発, 快活

W

- □ **wake up** 起きる, 目を覚ます
- □ **walk** 熟 go walking 散歩に出掛ける walk away 立ち去る, 遠ざかる walk out the door ドアの外に出る, どこかに行く walk past 通り過ぎる walk up 歩み寄る, 歩いて上る
- □ **wall** 熟 against the wall 壁を背にして
- □ **wash away** 押し流す
- □ **way** 熟 find one's way たどり着く in this way このようにして lead the way 先に立って導く, 案内する, 率先する make one's way 進む, 行く on one's way 途中で one's way to (~への) 途中で this way このように way out 出口, 逃げ道, 脱出方法
- □ **wedding** 名結婚式, 婚礼
- □ **weep** 動①しくしく泣く, 嘆き悲しむ ②しずくが垂れる
- □ **well** 熟 as well as ~と同様に
- □ **well-known** 形よく知られた, 有名な
- □ **what to make of** ~をどう判断するか
- □ **while** 熟 for a while しばらくの間, 少しの間
- □ **whisper** 動ささやく, 小声で話す 名ささやき, ひそひそ話, うわさ
- □ **white** 熟 turn white 青ざめる, 血の気が引く
- □ **whoever** 代 ~する人は誰でも, 誰が~しようとも
- □ **whole** 形全体の, すべての, 完全な, 満~, 丸~
- □ **whom** 代①誰を[に] ②《関係代名詞》~するところの人, そしてその人を
- □ **Why not?** どうしてだめなのですか。いいですとも。ぜひそうしよう!
- □ **wide** 形幅の広い, 広範囲の, 幅が~ある 副広く, 大きく開いて
- □ **wild** 熟 go wild 狂乱する
- □ **wildly** 副荒々しく, 乱暴に, むやみに
- □ **will have done** ~してしまっているだろう《未来完了形》
- □ **win over** 説得する, 口説き落とす
- □ **wine** 名ワイン, ぶどう酒
- □ **witness** 動目撃する
- □ **wives** 名 wife (妻) の複数
- □ **woke** 動 wake (目が覚める) の過去
- □ **wonder** 動①不思議に思う, (~に) 驚く ②(~かしらと) 思う 名驚き(の念), 不思議なもの in wonder 驚いて
- □ **work of** ~の仕業
- □ **work on** ~に取り組む
- □ **worker** 名仕事をする人, 労働者
- □ **worried** 形心配そうな, 不安げな
- □ **would like to** ~したいと思う
- □ **write down** 書き留める
- □ **writing** 名①書くこと, 作文, 著述 ②筆跡 ③書き物, 書かれたもの, 文書
- □ **wrong with** 《be-》(~にとって) まずい点がある

English Conversational Ability Test
国際英語会話能力検定

● E-CATとは…
英語が話せるようになるための
テストです。インターネット
ベースで、30分であなたの発
話力をチェックします。

www.ecatexam.com

● iTEP®とは…
世界各国の企業、政府機関、アメリカの大学
300校以上が、英語能力判定テストとして採用。
オンラインによる90分のテストで文法、リー
ディング、リスニング、ライティング、スピー
キングの5技能をスコア化。iTEP®は、留学、就
職、海外赴任などに必要な、世界に通用する英
語力を総合的に評価する画期的なテストです。

www.itepexamjapan.com

ラダーシリーズ
The Phantom of the Opera　オペラ座の怪人

2015年2月6日　第1刷発行
2025年4月12日　第9刷発行

原著者　ガストン・ルルー

リライト　ニーナ・ウェグナー

発行者　賀川　洋

発行所　IBCパブリッシング株式会社
　　　　〒162-0804 東京都新宿区中里町29番3号
　　　　菱秀神楽坂ビル
　　　　Tel. 03-3513-4511　Fax. 03-3513-4512
　　　　www.ibcpub.co.jp

© IBC Publishing, Inc. 2015

印刷　株式会社シナノパブリッシングプレス
装丁　伊藤 理恵
組版データ　Cg Elante Regular + Sanvito Pro Semibold

落丁本・乱丁本は、小社宛にお送りください。送料小社負担にてお取り替えいたします。本書の無断複写（コピー）は著作権法上での例外を除き禁じられています。

Printed in Japan
ISBN978-4-7946-0323-4